College

Hiring
People

BEST PRACTICES:

Hiring People

RECRUIT AND KEEP
THE BRIGHTEST STARS

KATHY SHWIFF

Collins

An Imprint of HarperCollins*Publishers*

HarperCollins books may be purchased for educational,
business, or sales promotional use. For information,
please write: Special Markets Department, HarperCollins
Publishers, 10 East 53rd Street, New York, NY 10022.

Employment laws differ from state to state. The editors
recommend consulting your company's human resources
or legal department before taking any action regarding
employees.

Produced for HarperCollins by:

HYLAS PUBLISHING
129 MAIN STREET
IRVINGTON, NY 10533
WWW.HYLASPUBLISHING.COM

FIRST EDITION
Library of Congress Cataloguing-in-Publication Data has
been applied for.

ISBN: 978-0-06-114557-5

07 08 09 10 11   RRD   10 9 8 7 6 5 4 3 2 1

Kathy Shwiff is business editor at the *Daily Record,* a Gannett newspaper that covers Morris County, New Jersey. A native of Dallas, she earned bachelor's and law degrees at the University of Texas.

Contents

PREFACE   viii

1 STAR SEARCH: ATTRACTING TOP PERFORMERS   1

Describing the Job   3
Advertising the Position   11
Recruiting   29
Building a Referral Network   32
Job Fairs   41
Using Recruiters   42
Screening and Evaluating Resumes   47

2 INTERVIEWING   55

Preliminary Screening   56
Interviewing 101: The Basics   62
Checking Out Promising Prospects   87
The Final Decision   96

3 WELCOME ABOARD   **99**
   Crafting Your Offer   100
   Making the Offer   114
   Getting Off to a Good Start   121
   Retaining Employees   127
   When It Doesn't Work Out   130

   OFF AND RUNNING   **134**

   SOURCES   **138**

   RECOMMENDED READING   **140**

   INDEX   **146**

Preface

What is the best way to hire a perfect employee? Where is the most cost-effective place to advertise open positions? How do you write an ad that will attract a pool of strong candidates? How can you identify a star performer from a stack of resumes? Will asking interviewees about their past experiences predict their future performance in your company? What interview questions are legally out-of-bounds? How do you craft an appealing offer?

In this book, we distill the wisdom of some of the best minds in the field of human resources to help you hire talented employees with ease. The language is simple and the design colorful to make the information easy to grasp.

Quizzes help you assess your knowledge of the hiring process. Case files show how companies have addressed their own hiring challenges. Sidebars give you a big-picture look at hiring and highlight innovative, out-of-the-box solutions worth considering. Quotes from business leaders will motivate you as you begin looking for the perfect employee. Finally, in case you want to dig deeper into hiring and related management issues, we recommend some of the most important business books available. The authors of these books both influence and reflect today's thinking about effective hiring practices and related management issues. Understanding the ideas they cover will inspire you as a manager.

Even if you don't dip into these volumes, the knowledge you gain from studying the pages of this book will equip you to deal firmly, effectively, and insightfully with the hiring challenges you face regularly on the job—to help you improve your company and the lives of the people who support you.

THE EDITORS

STAR SEARCH: ATTRACTING TOP PERFORMERS

"No organization can do better than the people it has."

—Peter Drucker, management guru and author (1909–2005)

Filling your ranks with good people has never been more important. That's because your people represent your company to the public; and they're the ones who will create your success.

If you can get the right people onto your team, and if you then give them the freedom to think and be creative, they can work magic. Yet good people are in short supply. Although universities and business schools around the world are churning out tens of thousands of MBAs every year, the imminent retirement of a whole generation—the 76 million baby boomers—means a wave of positions will be vacant. The competition for the top talent is already stiff. Within the next ten years, it will become even more intense.

Whether the person you're hiring is a junior software developer or a senior project manager, a civil engineer or a newsletter editor, a hotel maid or a registered nurse, getting a star performer to notice the position you want to fill, to come in and talk to you, and to choose you over other companies demands increasing skill.

Smart managers need to develop every possible resource. They need to build networks of good people they can tap into when they have jobs to fill. They need to develop skills among interns. They need to raise their firm's visibility so that people will come to them. They need to discover talent in every corner of their communities, focusing on groups of people who may be underemployed—among them women, many of whom drop out of the workforce at some point in their careers and subsequently find it difficult to return. Managers need to create a diverse workforce to benefit from the competitive edge that results when diverse approaches to problems and diverse points of view are adopted.

Having invested so much time in developing talent pools, smart managers will need to figure out how to bring these stars in house. They'll need to respond quickly to applicants via phone calls, run intelligent interviews, and learn to sell the candidate on their company.

Searches are expensive, both in time and money, not to mention the productivity lost while a job sits vacant. So you need to do whatever it takes to make your hiring process quicker and more effective. It's simply good business.

The journey from deciding to bring the best possible people on board to actually making the hire can be long and difficult. It is punctuated by challenges: writing a clear job description, choosing the most effective (and most cost-effective) advertising medium, and crafting your listing so that it appeals to the kind of individual you hope to find. Although some people wait until they have a job opening to pursue candidates, it's a good idea to be on the lookout year-round. You may want to do some active recruiting, for instance. You will definitely want to build a list of people you might some day want to work with, so that you'll have a roster of people to interview as soon as the need arises.

DESCRIBING THE JOB

Let's suppose that you're losing a key member of your department. Or perhaps you've met a talented young person who you'd like to find a way to bring on board. One of the first things you need to tackle before you set the hiring process in motion is the job description.

The **BIG** Picture

PERSONALITY AND PASSION ARE A PLUS

When reviewing the basic requirements for a job, remember that character traits and personality matter as much as skills. Every hiring manager emphasizes a different set of attributes that he or she values.

Jack Welch, who led General Electric as CEO for 21 years and spent about half his time hiring and coaching his staff, valued integrity above all else. To him, it was essential that the people around him could be relied upon to tell the truth and to keep their word. Next, he looked for intelligence, curiosity, breadth of knowledge, maturity, and the ability to handle success as well as stress and setbacks with aplomb. Also important to him were people with

If you're starting with an existing position, pull the most recent description of the position held by your departing employee and determine whether it accurately describes the functions of the job. If the text hasn't been updated for a while, it may well need dusting off, especially if your company has had any reorganizations since it was last revisited.

Give careful thought to what the person in that position actually did, day in and day out. What were the key tasks that the individual performed?

positive energy, people who "thrive on action and relish change." He prized the capacity to motivate and energize others, "to inspire them to take on the impossible." He wanted people who could get a job done and people with what he called "edge"—that is, the courage to make hard decisions. Finally, he sought passion—"a heartfelt, deep, and authentic excitement about work."

Consider your company's mission and goals, and determine what personal qualities are necessary to help you work toward them. Then tailor your hiring process to uncover people with those qualities.

Source: *Winning* by Jack Welch (Collins, 2005).

What are your expectations as to productivity and quality? Is this a back-office kind of job, offering little contact with the public, or does the person in this job interact with customers, clients, or vendors outside the company?

What experience and skills are required to do the job? What training and education? What are the challenges and opportunities the job offers? Enlist the help of your departing employee or another employee in the same role when gathering all this information.

Outside the Box

TEN STEPS TO EXCELLENT HIRES

Harvey B. Mackay founded Mackay
Envelope Company at the age of 26
and proceeded to build it into a $100
million company. The following ten-
step program for filling jobs is based
on Mackay's own process for hiring
executives.

1. Candidate is first interviewed by
   human resources.

2. Managers company-wide conduct
   follow-up interviews. These managers then compare notes and make
   recommendations.

3. Hiring manager meets with candidate for a 30-minute interview.
   Midway through, he or she asks for
   the name of a mentor or influential
   teacher who knows the candidate
   well and calls this person.

4. Hiring manager follows up with a
   30-minute phone conversation to
   determine the candidate's ability
   to project and communicate by
   telephone.

5. Industry people who may have come into contact with the candidate are called.

6. Candidate is interviewed at home.

7. Hiring manager socializes with the candidate and his or her significant other at a concert, theater, or movie. This step is especially important for salespeople, who may be seeing customers socially.

8. Peers in noncompeting companies are briefly interviewed.

9. Hiring manager has a conversation with the in-house person who is most knowledgeable in the candidate's skill area—controller, purchasing agent, or the like.

10. Company psychologist or human resources person is consulted.

This rigorous process not only yields staff members who are a good fit—and who stay for years—it also enforces a sense of pride among existing staff at being part of such a select company.

SOURCE: *Swim with the Sharks without Being Eaten Alive* (Reissue Edition) by Harvey B. Mackay (Collins, 2005).

If you're going to add to your head count, brainstorm the many tasks and roles you anticipate that an employee may undertake in this new job. Again, consider your productivity and quality expectations.

It's vital to have an accurate job description so that you and your new employee have a shared understanding of what's expected of him or her. Moreover, writing a job description helps you clarify your thinking, set pay ranges, plan interview questions, and—after you have made the hire—evaluate the new employee's performance.

When you craft the job description, you may also become aware of other job descriptions in your department that need revision.

The Basics of Job Descriptions

A good job description covers all the parameters of the position. It is detailed and specific, but also loose enough to allow the employee to grow with the job. Be concise and use language that can be readily understood by the general public. Don't use idiosyncratic terms specific to your organization, or mention internal divisions that change frequently or wouldn't be readily recognized outside the organization.

The job description should include these elements: the title of the position, a job summary, a list of key responsibilities, a statement of the minimum job requirements, certifications or licenses needed, physical requirements, a disclaimer, and details of hours and salary ranges.

The job title you post should ideally be a shortened version of the actual title—"graphic

CASE *FILE*

RETENTION BEGINS WITH THE RIGHT PERSONALITY

In a 2005 National Restaurant Association study, restaurateurs called recruiting and retaining employees their biggest challenge. Not surprising, considering that the median length of employment for food-service workers is less than two years—half that of other industries.

Managers at Nick's Pizza & Pub in suburban Chicago have learned that instilling a positive attitude can make all the difference. They believe that while they can teach applicants how to do a job, candidates' personalities can't be changed. Once hired, all Nick's employees go through four days of paid orientation.

Rudy Miick, founder of Miick & Associates, a restaurant consulting company helping Nick's with staffing issues, says, "If we raise the bar of expectations, tell them clearly what's expected, treat them with respect, and train them well, we end up with a waiting line of people trying to get in the door."

Source: "Being the Boss" by Karen Springer, *Newsweek.com* (August 5, 2005).

designer," as opposed to "graphic designer for educational book division." You can fill in the details later in your ad. The title should also reflect the various duties of the position, "filing clerk/typist," for instance, and specify a level of skill required, "junior accountant" or "lead programmer." Don't inflate job titles to make them sound more important—opt for "assistant librarian" rather than "information resource technician." Avoid any titles that might refer to age, gender, or race.

The job summary should provide the basic requirements of the job; it can be concise or go into greater detail depending on the space available.

Focus on the key responsibilities of the job, listing the ones you feel are most critical and at which a desirable candidate will excel. Use action verbs, such as "implements" or "oversees" at the start of each item, and also explain where and how often tasks are to be done. Include the range of responsibilities, including financial and budgetary ones, and be sure to mention if the job includes supervisory responsibilities.

Indicate what the minimum job requirements are for the position. These might include personality and character traits; minimum educational requirements; minimum amount of experience; willingness to travel; and special skills, including fluency in a language or familiarity with specific computer software. Try to frame your description in objective, measurable terms. An ad that fits this criteria might read, "Resourceful college graduate with two years of marketing experience to do complex spreadsheets in Microsoft Excel, some knowledge of Spanish a plus."

If applicable, state your requirements for any certifications and licenses the job will require. Some industries are legally bound by licensing restrictions, so make sure you know whether a worker at your firm needs a practitioner's license or a license to operate heavy machinery, etc.

Describe the physical requirements of the job, if any, such as lifting heavy objects or standing for long periods of time.

It's important to include a disclaimer that clearly states that the description outlines only the typical responsibilities of the job, and not all the duties that the employee will be required to perform. Leave room for yourself to assign other duties if the need arises. For instance, you might write "Job involves an additional variety of tasks with plenty of room for growth."

When describing required working hours and salary, specify whether a job is full time or part time, and detail the range of compensation. Don't forget to highlight your company's benefits plan and other perks. For example, "Full-time position, starting in the low $40s with full medical and dental coverage plus a 401K."

ADVERTISING THE POSITION

Once you've decided what type of person the job requires, it's time to start looking. If you're lucky, the right person will walk through the door, resume in hand, hoping to work for your company. But it doesn't often happen that way. Most likely, you'll have to engage your company's human resources department. If you handle human resources yourself, prepare for some decisions. Right off the bat, you have to figure out how to spread the word that you're searching for a new employee.

There are so many places to spend your candidate-recruiting dollars that it's hard to know where to go first. Traditionally, employers have used classified ads or staffing firms to fill hourly jobs; display ads in newspapers and industry-specific journals as well as staffing firms to fill low- to mid-range professional jobs; and executive search firms to fill senior professional and managerial positions. And these approaches still make a lot of sense. According to an article at Clickz.com, the statistics from a 2005 TNS Survey for The Conference Board suggest that most job seekers with incomes lower than $25,000 still rely on newspapers, and only half of them use the Internet. Therefore, when you're trying to fill entry-level and lower-wage positions, you are likely to reach all the potential applicants you need through your local paper.

On the other hand, the Internet has become a major recruiting channel: The same study revealed that three-quarters of people under 35 and people with higher incomes use the Internet. The Web is home to a fast-proliferating number of job boards, including sprawling sites with thousands of listings, and niche job boards aimed at particular segments of job hunters.

If you are seeking talented young candidates, online advertising is quick and easy. Many job

Outside the Box

BUILDING DIVERSITY

"You can't build a great company without great people, and great people are not just white, straight men aged 25 to 40," Joe Gregory, president of Lehman Brothers, told the *New York Times*. To build a diverse work force that brings a variety of points of view to the problems of your business, consider doing the following:

- Advertise in publications read by the individuals you want to attract.

- If you use a recruiter, let the recruiter know you are interested in building a diverse workforce.

- Create employee groups for women, gays, and racial and ethnic minorities to signal your company's interest in minorities.

- Look for clues to a person's minority status in a resume. These include academic connections, professional activities, and civic or employment-related committees that are minority-related.

SOURCE: "The Fork in the Road" by Jenny Anderson, *New York Times* (August 6, 2006).

boards require nothing more of you than an e-mail address and an Internet connection. Local and national resume databases offer a huge pool of candidates. Because space is not as tight as it is for print ads, you have room to talk up the benefits of the job or aspects of your company's culture that might appeal to job-seekers. Major career boards also work to ensure that the database is up to date and offer profiles of candidates actively looking for positions.

> "Talent: Attract it. Nurture it. Mentor it. Reward it. Create the context in which it can thrive."
>
> —Thomas J. Peters, coauthor of *In Search of Excellence*

In addition, database management tools such as PCRecruiter, Resume Direct, and Black Dog Recruiting allow you to track where you are in the hiring process. Check online under keywords "database management, hiring and recruiting" for a list of current software products to help you manage your recruiting process.

CASE *FILE*

HIRING FROM WITHIN

It's not every CEO who mixes with the rank and file—and likes it—but Tony Fernandes does just that. The visionary founder of AirAsia, Asia's first low-cost carrier, Fernandes insists his most satisfying experiences as a manager are when he can "get close to the operation." Whether it's carrying bags with the luggage handlers or helping out at the check-in counter, he places a premium on getting to know his staff. He recently opened a cadet pilot program to all his employees, many of whom, he felt, "had the brains but just didn't have the money to get an education." When the first group of cadets graduated, 11 out of 19 came from within the company, something the other employees certainly noted. Fernandes said, "There was one kid who joined us to carry bags, and 18 months later he was a First Officer of a 737. Can you imagine what that does for the motivation in the company? Everyone talks about developing human capital, but we did it."

SOURCE: "Changing Top Down Culture Among Managers in Asia" by Cris Prystay, CareerJournal.com (May 30, 2006).

Print and Electronic Options

When developing an advertising program for recruiting, your goal should be to attract the most qualified candidates for the money you have to spend. In this light, Internet advertising is very appealing. Job postings on the Internet and online resume database searches cost considerably less than newspaper ads and the services of staffing or recruiting firms. As job sites compete with one another, the price of online job listings continues to decline, and traditional newspaper ads are becoming even more expensive by comparison.

In general, the more people who will see your job advertising, the more you will pay to place it. Every firm has a different take on the most productive way to advertise. The best course is to think carefully about the type of people you want to attract and choose the method most likely to reach them. That way you won't be wasting your recruiting dollars speaking to people who can't do the job. To draw the widest range of applicants, advertise in a variety of media.

Advertising in major city daily papers is the traditional way to recruit employees. Job seekers like combing these newspapers for opportunities—scanning the wide range of jobs spread out in front of them, drawing circles around those that interest them, and crossing out those to which they've already responded. To advertise a job locally, think about running a classified ad in shoppers and weekly newspapers, the publication of the chamber of commerce, or a town newsletter. You may also want to post openings

Behind the Numbers

WHERE ARE PEOPLE LOOKING FOR JOBS?

A 2006 Conference Board survey of 5000 households reports that 70 percent of job seekers currently rely on both the Web and newspapers. Not only has the Internet become an accepted source of job information, the survey also indicated that of the people who received offers (48 percent), the largest share (38 percent) linked these offers to using the Web. Other job seekers cited networking and employment agencies, roughly 30 percent each, with newspaper searches generating only 24 percent of offers.

SOURCE: "Help Wanted Ads" Larry Swisher, *BNA Daily Labor Report* (November 8, 2006).

on community, high school, and college or university bulletin boards.

If you're searching for a professional with very specific skills, it may be more cost-efficient to advertise in a specialized Web site or publication. For example, theater companies in New York often advertise auditions for actors in the magazine *Backstage,* which is dedicated to acting and the theater.

Posting job openings on the Internet is not only cost effective, it can produce results in a matter of hours, often cutting the time it takes to fill a position by days, if not weeks. Consider

CASE *FILE*

THE PERSONAL TOUCH

Talk about a hiring boom—in April of 2006 Starbucks was placing new people at the rate of 200 a day. With its eventual goal of opening 30,000 stores worldwide, the java giant is faced with recruiting employees in the tens of thousands.

In an effort to maintain the distinctive Starbuck's aura and avoid cookie-cutter hiring, Starbucks' recruiters have begun adding personal touches to interviews—a coffee-tasting session with an applicant and staff is a fairly common occurrence. The company also has a "candidates' bill of rights" that prompts recruiters to call or send handwritten notes to applicants rather than form letters. It also establishes guidelines for how quickly applicants should hear back after an interview and urges recruiters to send out complimentary Starbucks gift cards, even when the candidate doesn't get the job.

SOURCE: "To Hire Sharp Employees, Recruit in Sharp Ways" by William C. Taylor, *New York Times* (April 23, 2006).

advertising on one of the mega job sites, such as CareerBuilder.com and Monster.com—which in 2006 accounted for 22.8 percent of Internet hires. Also consider posting job openings on specialized boards such as TheLadders.com, geared toward professionals earning $100,000 or more; HBS Tech Jobs, a niche site aimed at graduates from top MBA programs; and SnagAJob.com, which lists hourly and part-time jobs at places such as Home Depot, Wendy's, and Bed, Bath & Beyond.

It's not uncommon for the larger job sites to offer employers services in addition to listings. Careerbuilders.com, for example, allows you to "test drive" their resume database and review potential candidates' resumes before you agree to contract with them. HeadlessHunter.com and eBullpen.com use referrals and personality questionnaires to match applicants with employers. When choosing among the many places to advertise job openings, it helps to ask other people in your business or industry for their hiring success stories. Check out sites such as CareerXroads.com and Weddles.com, which cover the job-boards industry.

When advertising on the Internet, don't forget about your company's own Web site. Adding a "Careers" section to your corporate site is a wise move—it offers a permanent recruiting space, plus many job seekers target specific companies and frequently check for openings on their sites.

Another good tactic is recruiting through the Web sites of professional associations, or trade organizations such as the American Institute of Certified Public Accountants. While people

Dos & Don'ts ☑

TARGETING THE TALENT YOU NEED

Before placing your ad or job listing in any media, review the following tips and suggestions:

- ☐ Do review the job description to clarify the qualities you want in a successful candidate.

- ☐ Do evaluate where the right candidates or talent for your position typically search for job listings.

- ☐ Don't overlook candidates who may not be actively looking for a new opportunity; reach them by advertising on industry-related sites and sites unrelated to work.

not actively looking for jobs are unlikely to visit employer sites or big job boards, they probably check out specialty sites in order to network with their peers, or read about issues in their field, and they might take a look at job postings there. If you are hiring in a field that has a strong professional or trade association, it makes sense to post your job opening on their Web site.

Costs of Advertising

When deciding where to advertise, cost is always an important factor. But you will also want to

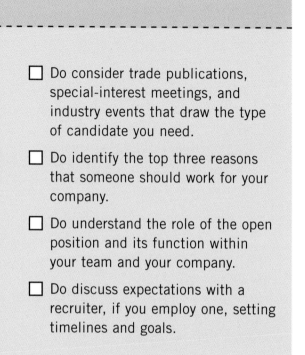

☐ Do consider trade publications, special-interest meetings, and industry events that draw the type of candidate you need.

☐ Do identify the top three reasons that someone should work for your company.

☐ Do understand the role of the open position and its function within your team and your company.

☐ Do discuss expectations with a recruiter, if you employ one, setting timelines and goals.

think about what you're getting for your money. Many of the largest job sites can be expensive, but they come with a proven track record. If you are looking for a versatile, multifaceted worker, then casting a broad net on one of these sites is a good idea. On the other hand, if you are seeking someone with very specialized skills, try a smaller, less expensive niche site, such as an industry- or location-specific job site, or the Web site of a professional or industry association.

Before you consider posting on a Web site, you need to do a bit of investigation. What does

Behind the Numbers

WHERE ARE COMPANIES FINDING THE BEST CANDIDATES?

A 2005 survey of seventy-three leading employers ranked various sources of job candidates based on the percentage of organizations that reported being satisfied with the return on their investment.

Employee referrals	82%
Organization's Web site	71%
Campus recruiting	60%
Niche job boards	58%
General job boards	51%
Search firms	42%
Networking technology	36%
Commercial resume databases	33%
Career fairs	30%
Newspapers	15%

Source: "2006 Recruiting Trends Survey," Direct Employers/Booz Allen Hamilton (January 2006).

it cost to advertise a job? How many people visit the site each month? How many and what percentage of these are in the group you're targeting? Since you want people to actually find your ad, look into job boards that can tell you how long people stay on their site. Also, ask when the site was founded. The longer it's been in business, the more information you have on its reliability and performance. Also, find out what the site does to draw in passive job seekers. Are there features and activities specifically designed to appeal to people who aren't looking for a job, such as discussion groups or articles about improving on-the-job performance?

The length of time that listings remain posted varies from site to site, so ask how long your ad will be up. The longer the better. There are also some sites that will let you test-drive their database—offering you one free perusal, or giving you limited access for a set price. Also, you need to know if companies that pay a premium get preferential placement. In that case, your ad might fall to the bottom of the list—meaning fewer people will see your listing.

The cost of Internet listings varies widely, depending on your specific needs. Although some Web sites have introduced pay-for-performance pricing, similar to Google's practice of charging advertisers a certain amount for each person who clicks on their ads, that method usually doesn't work with recruitment ads—the best job candidates are not necessarily those clicking on your ad, so you shouldn't have to pay for those random hits.

For print ads, either in newspapers or trade magazines, you usually pay by the word or by the line. Larger display ads, or those with special attention-getting design elements typically cost more. On the other hand, your local weekly newspaper or shopper can often be a bargain if you don't mind restricting your candidate pool to people in your local area.

Writing Your Ad

The quality of your ad makes a big difference to how much response it will generate. Before you sit down to write, however, survey other listings for similar jobs in the sites or publications in which you plan to advertise. This will give you an idea of what other companies are doing to attract people with the same skills and how much they are paying in wages and benefits.

Your ad needs to be livelier than the competition's. Grab the attention not just of serious job seekers, the people who are aggressively searching for a new position, but also of people who may not be completely happy with their current job and are browsing the classifieds to see what's out there.

Think about what kind of person you're seeking, and anticipate what might interest that individual in your company. Determine what's outstanding about this particular job? Where does its appeal lie? The pay? The benefits? Its fast pace? Opportunity for advancement? It's a good idea to succinctly state the most appealing aspects of the job up front. Then add the basic details of the job description described in the section above: title, qualifications and experience, salary or pay range, a note about any benefits that you offer, such as a 401(k), medical, or dental plans, and your contact information.

If you have also listed the job online, give the URL in the print ad, and if you have a job ID

Outside the Box

HOW TO CHOOSE

When trying to fill a position, companies tend to look for a candidate whose last job, or next-to-last job, was an exact copy of the one they're trying to fill. However, some of the best minds in American business today don't agree with this method. Instead, they advise focusing not on a candidate's past job experience but on their qualities and skills. Ask yourself, does the job call for a great deal of problem solving? Will the employee have lots of autonomy? Are the things your people learn on the job more important than the things they bring to the job? Must they be able to learn and adapt quickly? When the answer to all these questions is "yes," the authors of *It's Not the Big That Eat the Small . . .* advise managers to concentrate on hiring someone with the right attitude—whether or not that individual has the matching experience. "Proven initiative" is what they are after—people with ingenuity and resilience, as well as a track record of overcoming hardships.

SOURCE: *It's Not the Big That Eat the Small . . . It's the Fast That Eat the Slow* by Jason Jennings and Laurence Haughton (HarperBusiness, 2002).

Dos & Don'ts ☑

HOW TO WRITE A GOOD ONLINE AD

It takes skill to craft an effective ad for an Internet site. You want to appeal not only to active job seekers but also to those who are just testing the waters by checking employment sites, so-called "passive job seekers." To make your ad appealing to both types of online job seekers, keep these tips in mind:

☐ Do include terms that convey urgency, such as "Immediate Opening" or "Available Now."

☐ Do use a punchy, creative teaser, such as "Innovative Thinkers Wanted."

☐ Do place salary and/or benefits near the top of the ad; surveys have shown that this increases the number of respondents.

☐ Don't use job titles that are unclear or idiosyncratic to your company.

or ad codes, note them as well. Because you are not paying by the word or line, online ads can afford to be more discursive. Instead of having to describe the job succinctly, you have as many

☐ Do provide a bulleted list of required skills; describe these skills in terms that are likely to be used by candidates as keywords in a search engine.

☐ Don't abbreviate words, since online ad space is not restricted. Also, an abbreviation might not show up in a job hunter's keyword search.

☐ Do include information about career advancement at your company.

☐ Do include information about your work environment, any unusual benefits, and intangibles that set the company apart.

☐ Don't forget to specify your location—city, state, and region.

☐ Do add a link to community Web pages describing the local lifestyle.

as 100 words to describe why your opening is a dream job and why your company is a dream employer. The rest of the space can be given over to other essentials, including a statement of your commitment to protecting the candidate's privacy and a more detailed description of what the job involves, again in terms designed to appeal to your ideal candidate. If your company's Web site

CASE *FILE*

BRING ON (FLY IN) THE CANDIDATES!

Continental Airlines has developed an efficient global hiring strategy that eliminates local recruiters and centralizes the process. When the airline begins service to a new international destination, it announces in local media that it will be hiring and then guides people to its Web site, where job openings are posted. Once there, candidates are required to answer questions related to the job they are seeking before they can fill out an application. Based on their responses, they are either culled automatically or allowed to move on. If an application is accepted, the candidate is flown to Continental headquarters for interviews. The U.S.-based recruiting staff does not travel to conduct interviews locally. Thus, the company is able to process more than 80,000 international applications annually.

SOURCE: "Paperless Route for Recruiting" by Fay Hanson, Workforce.com (February 27, 2006).

RESPONDING TO RESUMES

Once you've made your resume selection, make a point of responding to every application, sooner rather than later. The best candidates will naturally be in demand, so you don't want to lose a great hire just because you didn't get back to her quickly enough.

Personal responses are preferable, but even a form letter telling job seekers that their resumes are in your hands is acceptable.

THE BOTTOM LINE

includes an employment section, link to it: Your online ad will be more effective if prospective employees can contact you directly or go straight from the ad to an online job application. Laura Sewell of WetFeet.com suggests also offering an overview in your ad of how you process online applications and how long the processing takes.

Finally, give applicants a way to follow up with someone in person, whether it is the name and phone number of the hiring manager, or a general e-mail account for employment inquiries.

RECRUITING

When you have a specific position to fill, advertising in print or on the Web is a perfectly legitimate way to attract talent. Yet smart employers never stop looking for good people, and they use all the means at their disposal.

For most companies, their Web site is their key recruiting tool. Advertising openings on your own site works especially well if your company is recognized and sought after as an employer. In order to effectively attract job candidates, the site must be easy to use. Place a prominent link to the career section on the company's home page. Include links to career-related information, such as job listings, facts about compensation levels and your benefit structure, and a sketch of the company's history and culture.

Convince browsing candidates why they should come work for the company. Include accurate information about opportunities for advancement, and give them the tools they will need during the recruitment process, such as the recruiters' name, title, and contact information, office locations, and information about how you choose among applicants. Finally, provide an online application. By gathering basic information abut the candidate, asking a few key questions, and capturing the candidate's application electronically, you can build a valuable talent database.

Keep the content of your Web site accurate and up-to-date. When company rosters change or new branches open, revise Web pages as appropriate. There should be fresh content on the pages that attract the most traffic. Look for links that don't work. If possible, speed up the time it takes to search job openings and upload a resume. Regularly road test your Web site from the job seeker's point of view.

Visitors should be able to access your job listings easily. Let people browse jobs without registering.

The **BIG** Picture

BUILDING A REPUTATION

Some companies don't have to advertise openings. Their reputation as a great place to work precedes them, and they often get unsolicited resumes. If you're not getting your share of those, make it part of your recruiting strategy to raise general awareness of your company. Mark Nowlan, a columnist at Entrepreneur.com, advises small businesses that want to raise their visibility to issue news releases to publications read by the people they're trying to reach. While you can distribute news releases yourself, the most reliable way to broadcast news about your company is to use a newswire service, such as BusinessWire or PR News, Nowlan says.

Even when your business is not making news, your executives can become known as experts by making themselves available to reporters looking for experts to quote in articles about industry trends.

Make the application process simple and include a function that lets people e-mail job listings to friends. Build in the capacity to search by job category, by keywords, and, if appropriate, by job location. You may want to have a separate section for college recruitment. Many cutting-edge corporate Web sites give applicants a choice of various methods for submitting their resumes—in a word-processing document or PDF file; by cutting and pasting it into an online application; or by a resume builder. These sites also allow candidates the option of storing their resume or profile.

BUILDING A REFERRAL NETWORK

A surprising number of job seekers land their positions by networking with friends and family. Finding new employees through such referrals has many advantages, not the least of

> "Employee referrals are the single best way to find more top people... At least 50 percent of the people you hire should come from this group."
>
> —Lou Adler,
> author of *Hire With Your Head*

IMPROVING YOUR
EMPLOYEE-REFERRAL PROGRAM

Dave Lefkow, the senior director of strategic partnerships at Jobster, has several suggestions for improving your employee referral program. He first recommends setting measurable goals, such as increasing the number of hires from employee referrals by a specific percentage.

Second, announce the details of your program online and include the guidelines and forms. Third, offer rewards. Although cash awards are popular, some small companies give T-shirts, personal organizers, and other items for referrals.

Finally, continue to promote your referral program, as well as any new job openings, through e-mails, an online newsletter, and other company publications. Don't forget that new hires can be a good source of referrals—they all have friends and business contacts from their previous jobs.

SOURCE: "Improving your Employee Referral Program and Justifying your Investment" by Dave Lefkow, Ere.net (February 21, 2002).

THE BOTTOM LINE

which is cost. Beyond that, many companies find that new employees who come to them through networking with current employees are more qualified and have a low turnover rate.

Start publicizing job openings with the people who know your business best—your employees, customers, and suppliers. Asking customers to help you find talented employees shows that you value their opinions and can be a good way to strengthen your relationship. Your suppliers also have an interest in your success, because it could result in more business for them. Therefore, they are likely to go out of their way to help you find good job candidates.

Employee Referrals

One of the most cost-effective and efficient ways to recruit candidates is through your own employees. They have a vested interest in the success of your company and are unlikely to recommend people they wouldn't want to work with.

Because these referrals tend to yield such strong candidates, an increasing number of companies have instituted referral reward programs, offering money or other incentives. For instance, Gail Repsher Emery reported in *Washington Technology* that SRA International, a technology-consulting firm in Fairfax, Virginia, began awarding employees $500 when someone they recommended was hired. As a result, 40 percent of the company's new hires have been referred through employees. If your company currently has such a program, make sure your people know how to make a referral and what the rules and rewards are.

Whether or not you hire a referral, follow up with the referring employee. If you don't, you may find your staff much less likely to recommend another friend. Remember, a strong

Outside the Box

REACHING OUT TO EMPLOYEES

Traditional employee-referral recruitment efforts encourage workers to recommend family and friends. International pharmaceutical firm Eli Lilly & Company recently developed a three-part strategy to recruit more aggressively. Current employees are invited to human resource roundtables, where they identify the top performers in their field, after which human resources designates an individual to reach out to each of them. When a new employee comes aboard, they also are asked to list the best people they've worked with, and someone is assigned to make contact with them. Lilly's third step is to invite supervisors to "share your Rolodex" meetings, where they are encouraged to recruit strong prospects from their networks outside the company.

SOURCE: "What's Wrong with Employee Referral Programs?" by Peter D. Weddle, CareerJournal.com (September 19, 2005).

referral program turns every employee into a recruiter for you. But running such a program takes time, manpower, and a budget. At some larger companies, dedicated employee-referral recruiting teams investigate each person who is referred. Depending on your company's size, you might find yourself doing a lot of the legwork yourself during the referral process—yet the rewards could be worth it.

Alumni Referrals and Rehires

When employees leave a company on good terms to pursue other opportunities, it makes sense to stay in touch with them as another source of referrals. As Kate O'Sullivan reports in "Keeping in Touch" in *CFO Magazine,* Ernst & Young has a very successful program for returning employees, or "boomerangs," as the company refers to them.

You could initiate such a program in your company. Handle exit interviews with warmth and cordiality. Invite the employee to contact you when he or she makes a change down the road. Finally, stay in contact with all your alumni. Even if they don't come back, they may be able to send good candidates your way.

Internships

Taking advantage of your company's internship programs presents both you and your interns with a win-win proposition: The intern learns important job skills, while you gain a valuable resource for your department—and possibly a new hire if the intern proves worthy.

• POWER POINTS •

PLANNING FOR INTERNS

Providing interns the support they need makes all the difference. These are a few key things you can do to ensure the success of your internship program:

- Assign interns real work.

- Set measurable learning objectives.

- Provide detailed explanations of their assignments.

- Offer constructive feedback on their performance.

- Assign them to an experienced advisor with the time to teach and guide them.

- Give them the appropriate tools— desk, chair, phone, computer, or the like.

Now increasingly available both to high school students and to recent college graduates, internships have long been considered an essential adjunct of the college curriculum. They provide hands-on work experience that complements a course of study, build confidence, and help students put their abilities to

CASE *FILE*

CRUNCHING NUMBERS WITH INTERNS

At PricewaterhouseCoopers, the world's largest professional-services firm, interns don't simply report for work. They start out in Landsdown, Virginia, with a challenging week-and-a-half "boot camp." Recruits—that is, interns—tough it out together for long hours every day. Once on the job, interns are given older mentors as well as peer group mentors. They learn critical skills as members of client teams, including developing strategies and doing financial analysis.

Another auditing and accounting giant, Ernst & Young, specifically recruits interns who possess the same values as their employees—the desire to pursue professionalism in all matters. As a result, 90 percent of their interns become full-time employees.

SOURCE: "They Love It Here, and Here and Here," *BusinessWeek Online* (June 4, 2006).

the test. Consequently, a good internship—for a reputable company or one with strong learning opportunities—is highly sought after. As an indication of just how strong their appeal can be, consider the New York Yankees, who get more than 4,000 internship applications for just 20 positions.

Outside the Box

CREATING "GAME" COMPETITORS

In an effort to attract the nation's top young talent, a number of companies, such as L'Oreal, began sponsoring competitions that involve business-simulation games. By emphasizing such qualities as teamwork and problem-solving, these games pinpoint the outstanding candidates among participating undergraduates, graduate students, and MBAs.

L'Oreal offers three separate games, each with a different focus: e-Strat Challenge, a marketing strategy game; Brandstorm, in which students become marketing managers for Lancôme; and Ingenious, which requires students to oversee an engineering project. So far, the company's efforts have paid off: In 2006, according to Ronald Alsop in the *Wall Street Journal,* e-Strat Challenge, "attracted almost 40,000 students from 1,000 schools in 125 countries." Brandstorm has generated approximately 350 L'Oreal hires and interns, e-Strat generated another 200, and Ingenius has resulted in 36.

SOURCE: "Recruiters Are Using Games to Assess MBAs" by Ronald Alsop, *Wall Street Journal Online* (August 8, 2006).

For employers, internships hold comparable appeal, not the least because of the fresh ideas and positive energy interns supply, which can boost employee morale and motivation. Interns are not jaded; they're often thrilled to lend a hand. They can do research or support marketing efforts that will help you launch projects that have been on the back burner. By shouldering lower-level work, interns can also make your existing staff more productive. At the same time, employees overseeing interns can gain supervisory experience and improve project-management skills. Interns can boost the diversity of your work force, build relationships with schools and colleges, and increase your company's visibility among other students, who will soon enter the work force. Offering an internship also allows you to try out a young employee before bringing him or her permanently on board.

Internships can last from one month to one year, although a semester is average. Some students earn academic credit and some don't. Some earn a salary and others work for free. Internships at the U.S. Supreme Court, for instance, are non-paid. Some companies offer non-monetary perks, such as housing, free products, time with CEOs, or invitations to special events.

When creating your own internship program, remember that the best internships provide substantive work for the interns, so that they make a contribution even as they're building their skills. A good internship program should involve interns in day-to-day operations and expose them to different aspects of your company.

Start by asking your employees to come up with a list of jobs that interns could tackle—think of all those projects you've been too shorthanded to accomplish. Establish the expectation among your staff that interns will benefit the company and do meaningful work.

Designate one person on your staff to be in charge of the program and to manage the interns. Expect that they will spend three to four hours a week supervising one or two interns, and block out an additional two hours for each additional intern. When deciding how many interns to hire, factor in supervisory time, the amount of work you can assign, and the resources you'll need. Students may work 15 to 20 hours a week during fall and spring semesters and full-time in summer. Set aside adequate work space with access to computers and other equipment. Be sure to budget funds for recruitment, compensation, and incentives and rewards.

It's important to treat an intern as more than just the office grunt. Make sure that no more than 25 percent of the intern's time is spent on duties of a clerical or repetitive nature, such as selling, stock-keeping, telemarketing, or data entry. Some colleges and universities, especially those that offer academic credit for internships, require that employers sign a written agreement outlining measurable learning objectives.

JOB FAIRS

For smaller businesses, local job fairs are often a good source of candidates. They allow you to develop a list of people you might want to consider for internships and full-time jobs, and they have the advantage of letting you match a face to a resume. Cabrillo College offers the following "employer tips" to job fair recruiters:

- Make sure to set up your booth or table early, and be prepared with your presentation when the fair opens—the most motivated people are likely to be the first to arrive.
- Anticipate problems such as broken video equipment or missing electrical extension cords.
- Have brochures to hand out, but remember that people's impression of your organization will be based on their interaction with you.
- Always remain standing to convey a sense of excitement and a warm welcome. Don't wait for visitors to approach you—have someone with handouts to greet people.
- Be assertive and friendly when giving your pitch.
- Once you have a visitor's attention, keep your introduction or demonstration short and simple.
- After the fair, respond to all inquiries as soon as you can to reinforce your professional image.

USING RECRUITERS

Finding and evaluating potential employees takes a lot of time and energy, so if you do not have the time yourself, or if your staff is not experienced in all aspects of the hiring process—consider using a professional third-party recruiter or headhunter. Recruiters not only have experience finding qualified candidates for their clients, they are also able to tap into a larger

STAR SEARCH: ATTRACTING STAR PERFORMERS

Plan B

EXEMPLARY WORKERS

When hiring, you'd do well to consider the merits of former military personnel. These men and women have technical skills and leadership qualities that are in short supply in the civilian work force. Veterans are especially valued for their character traits, such as being respectful and a good teamplayers, performing well under pressure, and conducting themselves with integrity.

Employers looking to expand the diversity of their workforce will find these numbers appealing: According to the Defense Department, "18 percent of active-duty personnel are African-Americans, 9 percent are Hispanic, and about 15 percent are women."

If you are interested in recruiting veterans, there are numerous online sources, such as The Compass Group, Bradley Morris, Inc., and the Destiny Group, which maintains a large database of people transitioning out of the military.

SOURCE: "Detroit Forum: Motor City Likes Veterans" by Eilene Zimmerman, *New York Times* (June 18, 2006).

network of job seekers, many of whom they've screened previously for other positions.

If you are concerned about spending corporate dollars for a job you could arguably do yourself, bear in mind that recruiters offer a full range of services. In addition to finding potential candidates, most firms will actually prep job seekers before presenting them, then solicit feedback from both parties afterwards to evaluate the interview. Recruiters are also in a position to perform more thorough reference checks. Once you've made a hiring decision, recruiters will help you prepare your offer, including the salary and benefits package. They can also guide the new employee through any transition difficulties. As you can see, with third-party recruiters, you get a lot of hiring bang for your buck.

There are two basic types of recruiters to consider: retainer firms, which are at least partially paid upfront and work on exclusive assignments, and contingency firms, which are paid only after successfully placing someone and rarely receive exclusive assignments. Whether or not a retained-search firm places a candidate, they still receive a monthly retainer fee, and as a result are typically used to find high-salary, executive-level candidates. Most will also observe a year-long moratorium on recruiting employees after placing them with your firm. Contingency firms, which are often faster and offer a larger number of candidates than retainer firms, are useful for filling lower-wage or midlevel positions.

Retained-search firm fees currently average about 25 percent of first-year compensation.

But always negotiate the recruiter's fee—especially if it is your first time using the firm. In such cases, the agency is likely to give you a better deal in the

RESULTS FIRST

During the late 1990s, when it was clearly a "seller's market" and skilled job seekers could virtually name their price, retained recruiters' fees averaged about one-third of a candidate's first-year compensation, according to an article in the *Wall Street Journal*'s CareerJournal.com. These days, however, corporations are more results-oriented; they are loath to pay retained recruiters for supplying candidates that might not make the grade. This has led to what is now called a "container" or "retingency" plan—paying retained firms only when they've met a specific goal. Charlie Polachi, president of Polachi & Co., a retained-search firm in Sherburne, Massachusetts, is seeing this change firsthand—some clients now ask for a list of potential candidates or interviewed candidates, or link their payments to a candidate receiving an offer.

SOURCE: "As Talent War Resumes, Recruiters Jump Hoops to Earn Their Fees" by Perri Capell, *CareerJournal.com* (May 3, 2005).

THE BOTTOM LINE

hope that you will use them again. In addition, ask for a guarantee—that is, if the candidate does not work to your satisfaction for at least 90 days, the recruiter will either find a replacement at no extra charge or return some or all of fee.

When you enlist the help of a recruiter, be sure the firm understands your company's culture and has a clear idea of what background, experience, and skills you're seeking in a candidate. See to it that the recruiter is able to meet with key staff members during the initial analysis of your needs. You also need to know how any confidential information exchanged during the search will be treated and whether the firm will observe a moratorium on recruiting from your company after a search—and for how long.

Many employers find that using a recruiter is well worth the money, especially when they are trying to fill a job that requires highly special- ized training or experience. Headhunters have more freedom to solicit employees who work for your competitors than you would. Also, because recruiters bring a different perspective to the hir- ing process, they can encourage you to consider candidates you might miss or rule out. Many have an in-depth knowledge of the technical qualifica- tions of positions in one or more specialty fields. And although the agency does most of the work, the final hiring decision remains with you.

The Association of Executive Search Consultants, a professional association of retained executive search firms, has created a Code of Ethics and Professional Practice Guidelines.

You can find the code, as well as a list of its members at www.aesc.org. The Directory of Executive Recruiters lists retainer and contingency firms by geographical location and business areas. You can also seek agency referrals from your local chamber of commerce, business associates, or networking groups. Ask for two to three references from companies and two to three from candidates they have placed and then check them out.

SCREENING AND EVALUATING RESUMES

When you advertise a job opening, you will most likely be flooded with resumes or job applications. To efficiently screen and assess candidates' skills—and to prevent stars from getting lost in a mountain of submissions—you must establish a process for evaluating resumes.

Evaluating Resumes and Job Applications

Resumes remain an essential tool for employers in screening job candidates, determining if the candidate is a good fit for the position, and deciding whether or not to go on to the next step, an interview.

Although resumes tell you only what the candidate wants you to know, they still reveal a great deal. What is the overall look of the resume? Sophisticated? Sloppy? The visual presentation is important. A resume for someone looking for a job as an art director should be creative, with an interesting choice of typography that would be inappropriate for, say, a young lawyer's resume. Organization is key, in that it tends to predict how the candidate would prepare written material to present to customers or clients. In fact, some say that the structure of the resume—or lack thereof—reveals the working of the candidate's mind.

When evaluating resumes, look for stability by assessing how long the candidate has stayed at each job. Traditionally, stability is defined as at least three or four years in the same job, although corporate mergers and economic trends such as outsourcing have cost many

Red Flags ✗◆

RESUME RED FLAGS

When dozens or even hundreds of resumes are piled on your desk, you need a way to narrow down your search. Here are a few things to watch for when weeding out candidates:

- Typos

- Misspelled words

- Grammatical mistakes and poor punctuation

- Outdated information

- A non-chronological organization or lack of dates, which could be an attempt to disguise either a history of job hopping or a long period of unemployment people their jobs and resulted in shorter tenures in each job. A series of lateral career moves could mean that the applicant has been willing to take on new responsibilities even without an increase in pay or status.

Progress and promotions in previous jobs is often a good sign. Look for statements of results—such as "introduced new processes that saved $1.5 million per year"—and for an indication that the candidate played a significant

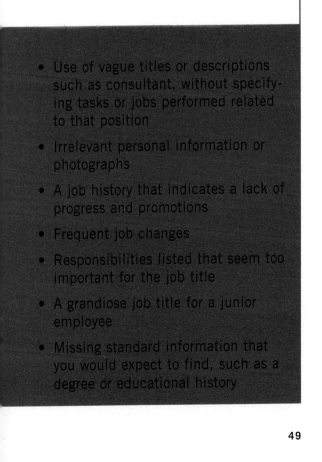

- Use of vague titles or descriptions such as consultant, without specifying tasks or jobs performed related to that position

- Irrelevant personal information or photographs

- A job history that indicates a lack of progress and promotions

- Frequent job changes

- Responsibilities listed that seem too important for the job title

- A grandiose job title for a junior employee

- Missing standard information that you would expect to find, such as a degree or educational history

RESUME REVELATIONS

A resume shows just what the candidate wants you to see, yet when you read between the lines, it can tell you a great deal about the candidate's skills, motivation, and character. The resume tells you much of what you need to know about a candidate:

Skills

- Has the candidate done this job elsewhere?

- Does he have the skills you require?

- Has he augmented his skills with on-the-job or outside training or classes?

- Did the candidate make a contribution with previous employers? Is he likely to do the same in your organization?

Character

- Does the candidate seem to have the energy and confidence to do the job?

- What is the evidence that she will be conscientious, hardworking, and determined?

- Did the candidate stay with previous employers for long periods of time?

- Does the evidence suggest the candidate will fit in and be a team player? Has she worked collaboratively in the past?

- Will she be easy to manage? Has she job-hopped, which might suggest issues with previous managers? Do coworkers rather than managers comprise her reference list?

- Will the company's management style and corporate culture suit her? Is the management style or culture of previous employers similar to your management style or company's culture or drastically different?

Salary expectations
- Is the job's salary range appropriate to his salary history?

- Is the salary what he wants or needs to earn?

- Do the benefits meet his needs?

- Can the company afford him?

THE BOTTOM LINE

role in achieving them. "Led," "planned," "coached," "collaborated," "coordinated," "motivated," "modernized," "negotiated," and similar action words highlight accomplishments; be sure that the accomplishments make sense in light of the candidate's level of seniority.

Functional resumes are organized according to skills used or functions fulfilled and might indicate job hopping or gaps in employment, particularly for highly qualified executives who may have been downsized. However, this type of organizational style is not necessarily a red flag: It can also be used to emphasize skills that a person hasn't used recently or to summarize the job history of individuals who have gained their experience in an assortment of diverse jobs.

Shaping Your Short List

If you have posted an opening on an electronic job board and are flooded with resumes and applications, you may feel overwhelmed. Many employers deal with the deluge by feeding the relevant information about the applicants into onsite databases that can be searched and sorted. These databases vary from sophisticated systems that use scanning, optical character recognition, and artificial intelligence, to simple systems that contain only manually entered information. Other companies enlist a resume storage service that stores information offsite. Larger companies may have hundreds of thousands of resumes in their database. If your company has such a data-base and if a human-resources staffer or other agent searches the database on your behalf, it's especially important for you to communicate your needs thoroughly. Depending on the time you have for the search, you may prefer to give your agent broader parameters, so that you can choose from a wider selection of candidates.

At this point—or if you don't have access to database search capability—you need to begin reviewing resumes and cover letters personally. As you do so, it's a good idea to review the job description once again. Then scan the submissions for indications that the candidate has the qualities and experience needed to do the job.

If spelling and writing proficiency and attention to detail are requirements, reject all those resumes with spelling mistakes and typos. The editor who claims to have "prooofread" at her previous job may not be the proofreader for you. If initiative and motivation are required, discard submissions that don't reveal specific interest in your company.

Some hiring experts recommend sorting resumes into three piles—the "nos," the "maybes," and the "must interviews." Chances are that this last stack will yield plenty of potential hires. If not, you can always sift through the "maybe" list one more time. Within your "must interview" group, either arrange the resumes in order of your interest or divide them into several subgroups based on your assessment of each candidate's potential.

Once you've reviewed all the available resumes and organized them according to their viability, it's time to move on to the next phase of the hiring process: the interview stage.

INTERVIEWING

"All the clever strategies and advanced technologies in the world are nowhere near as effective without great people to put them to work."

—Jack Welch,
former General Electric CEO and author of *Winning*

While resumes and cover letters present only the information that candidates want you to see, interviews allow you to find out about qualities or flaws that are not revealed on paper. Specifically, it is an opportunity to ask the questions that will help you assess how the candidate will perform on the job.

At the same time, you will be able to get a sense of whether the individual will thrive in your company culture. Finally, the interview allows you to articulate company values and to sell the candidate on the idea of joining your team.

It's vital to hone your interviewing skills and familiarize yourself with all aspects of the process. A badly handled interview can end up with a weak candidate making a deceptively strong impression, or send the perfect candidate running in the other direction, turned off by an unappealing manager or a job that was inadvertently portrayed as a dead end.

PRELIMINARY SCREENING

Some companies go straight from the stack of resumes to inviting candidates in. Interviewing is time consuming, however, so when the must-interview stack is large, you may want to do some preliminary screening, either through a phone interview or by using some type of quick assessment.

Phone Interviews

Consider screening candidates via a telephone interview before asking them in for a formal face-to-face interview. This is particularly helpful when you're interviewing candidates who live in a different geographic area and you want to avoid the costs (transportation and lodging expenses) of bringing an ill-suited candidate in for an interview.

Phone interviews should typically last between 10 to 30 minutes, so make every question count.

After all, this is your opportunity to determine whether the candidate has the minimum technical skills necessary to do the job. It might be helpful to jot down notes during the conversation, so you can refer to them later.

The BIG Picture

BEYOND DUE DILIGENCE

When Tom Peters and Robert H. Waterman, Jr., studied 43 of the best-run companies in the United States to explore what makes them successful, they found that one of the most important commonalities among these firms was their focus on people. Their hiring process, in particular, was intense, with many companies interviewing candidates as many as seven or eight times. The managers there wanted to get to know the people they were hiring—and to let the candidates get to know them as well. As these successful companies demonstrated, it pays off to take as much time as you need during the interview process to be sure the candidate is the right fit for the job and the organization.

SOURCE: *In Search of Excellence* by Thomas J. Peters and Robert H. Waterman, Jr. (HarperCollins, 1986).

Ask open-ended questions that reveal how well the candidate would fill the position and fit into the company as a whole, and attempt to gather as much information as you can, while keeping the tone light. Engage the candidate by listening carefully and asking follow-up questions, requesting clarification of statements you don't understand or asking for further explanations: How did she arrive at a specific decision? How did he feel about that outcome? Stay away from questions that can be answered with only a yes or a no.

> "If we didn't spend four hours on placing a man and placing him right, we'd spend 400 hours on cleaning up after our mistake."
>
> —Alfred Sloan,
> former president and CEO of General Motors
> (1875–1966)

After discussing the candidate's background and experience, go over salary requirements and assess the person's willingness to relocate, if necessary. Find out if the candidate will consent to background checks or drug testing, if required, and verify the candidate's availability and potential starting date.

Other Screening Methods

How a company prescreens depends largely on the nature of the job to be filled. Some larger companies eliminate candidates who don't meet

Behind the Numbers

LOOKING LONG AND HARD

A national study conducted by recruiting and staffing firm Spherion Corporation reports that hiring managers interview an average of 8 people for an available position. About 27 percent of smaller companies interview 10 or more people on average for an opening compared with only 14 percent of larger companies. Almost 42 percent of employers believe their managers are interviewing too many people. In an effort to reduce these numbers, more and more companies are turning to prescreening tools (51 percent of those surveyed) and assessment programs (60 percent) to find the most suitable candidates.

SOURCE: "The Spherion® Workforce® Study," Spherion Corporation. © 2006 Spherion Pacific Enterprises LLC.

• POWER POINTS •

WHAT'S IN A JOB APPLICATION?

The application is one of the best tools to screen job applicants. If your company doesn't already have a standard job application, it's easy to create one. There are a number of sites online, such as FindLegalForms. com, where you can download state-vetted templates and customize them for your own needs. Here is some of the information typically requested in applications:

- Candidate's name and contact information, including address, phone number, and e-mail address

- Education

requirements for the job by asking applicants to complete an application that covers basic information, for example, college degrees, visas, or a willingness to relocate. They purposely ask only a few questions and keep them brief to avoid driving away qualified candidates.

Many retailers and organizations that depend heavily on hourly workers have begun to prescreen using in-store automated systems. Automated-systems kiosks at stores such as Best Buy, Circuit City, and CVS give employers access

- Work experience, including salary levels and training

- Awards or honors received

- Special skills in languages or software

- Current employer contact information

- Position for which they are applying

- Desired salary

- Availability, i.e., when the applicant is ready to start

- Names and contact information for professional and personal references

to a large pool of applicants, help to quickly eliminate those who aren't suitable (for instance, applicants who are not willing to work nights and weekends), and even ask ethical questions (such as what individuals would do if they had observed a coworker stealing). This type of screening system allows a hiring manager to receive the job application within minutes, and the system even suggests interview questions targeted to that candidate. Some electronic screening tools store candidates' answers in a database, scoring and ranking them and comparing them against job requirements, then generating a short list of candidates, as well as a customized list of questions to ask each one.

Knowledge tests are another accepted method of prescreening. Many consulting firms, for instance, ask prospective employees to complete a short sample project. Magazine companies ask candidates to provide a list of ideas and to critique aspects of the magazine. Background checks or physical tests can also be used to prescreen applicants.

If you want to develop a preliminary assessment device of your own, based on the skills that will be needed on the job, think about instances in which a lack of a specific skill doomed previous employees to failure—and then figure out how you can test or assess whether a candidate possesses that skill without meeting him.

INTERVIEWING 101: THE BASICS

Once you've screened candidates—either via phone interviews, online questions, or by giving them a knowledge test to complete—you are ready to bring the best of the crop in for interviews. The goal of every interview is to assess the candidate's specific skills, to get a sense of how the person will fit in with your organization, and to judge the applicant's enthusiasm for the position. Determining whether the new employee will be handling specific tasks, supervising others, meeting with clients, or working independently will help you decide how to approach the interview. Varying the interview style, from informal to formal, as appropriate, can help highlight the candidate's qualities.

Decide on an interviewing plan from the outset. Ideally, if an applicant is to be interviewed by several managers, the same group should see all candidates. You could split the interviewing into two rounds, with one group handling initial interviews and another group interviewing only the most successful candidates. Or you could have some or all interviewers meet with a candidate more than once. Each person can ask the same questions, so you can compare notes, or different interviewers can probe different aspects

The **BIG** Picture

WHY YOU INTERVIEW PEOPLE

Richard Nelson Bolles, author of the phenomenally successful job-hunting manual *What Color Is Your Parachute?*, says that all interview questions are really addressing just four topics:

- Why are you here?

- What can you do for us?

- What kind of person are you (that is, honest, ethical, dependable, responsible)?

- Can we afford you?

SOURCE: *Managing for Dummies* by Bob Nelson and Peter Economy (Wiley, 2003).

of the candidate's skills and experience. It's best to coordinate the group's approach beforehand.

Use your job description and the list of skills, abilities, and behaviors required to do the job to

CASE *FILE*

RECRUITING FOR A VIRTUAL WORKPLACE

A full 70 percent of the employees at MySQL, a $40 million international software maker, work from home. Job applicants from all over the world are interviewed by phone and, to determine personality and work style, CEO Marten Mickos asks leading questions, such as, "How do you plan your day?" He knows he's on to something if they reply, "I always sleep until 11 A.M., then I start working." Mickos explains, "The brightest engineers like the calmness and coolness of the night," he says. On the other hand, he is wary of young men without family commitments or other distractions, people who will "read e-mails on their way to brush their teeth." The job can drive those people crazy, he warns.

Only at the end of the phone interview does he ask where the candidate lives.

SOURCE: "MySQL: Workers in 25 Countries with No HQ" by Josh Hyatt, *Fortune* (June 2006).

formulate a list of questions that will guide your discussion during the interview and elicit relevant information from the candidate. This technique not only ensures thorough and organized questioning; it also keeps your group's questions consistent from one interview to the next, if that's your intention.

It's critical for forming an objective opinion that all applicants be treated the same. At the end of each round of interviews, or at the end of the final interview, the management panel should get together to discuss the applicants and then rank them before making their decision.

Standard Interview Questions

Open your interview with an informal icebreaker to establish rapport and then offer some background information about the company and the position. You might start by telling the candidate your own history there and what the opportunities are in general at your firm. Then start asking questions.

Keep your questions open-ended, which will not only encourage candidates to talk, but will also demonstrate how well they think on their feet, something "yes" or "no" questions do not reveal. Avoid leading questions, or those that suggest what you want to hear. Be responsive and say things such as "I see," or "Tell me more," to urge the candidate to expand on answers. Paraphrase some answers to make sure you understand what the candidate is saying. But as a rule, you should allow the candidate to do most of the talking.

The **BIG** Picture

ASKING CANDIDATES TO BE CANDID

Former General Electric CEO Jack Welch believed that by far the most important questions to ask in an interview are, "Why did you leave your last job? And the one before that? And the one before that? Was it the environment? The boss? The team?" Here are some other key interview questions recommended by Martin E. Davis in his book *Managing a Small Business Made Easy:*

- What were your job responsibilities?

- What is it you like most—and least— about past jobs and your current job?

- What is your present compensation and benefits package?

- Why are you considering changing jobs?

- Are you aware of the responsibilities of the job you're applying for?

- What is the greatest strength you would bring to this position?

- What things do you find appealing about our company?

You can start by asking the candidate to say more about work experience and responsibilities listed on the resume and to give specifics:

- What do you think is your greatest challenge as a candidate for this position?

- What was your beginning compensation in your current job?

- What specific training have you had that might increase your ability to perform our job?

- In which school subjects were you most successful?

- Which subjects in school did you find the most difficult?

- Can you provide the names of coworkers who can vouch for your technical abilities? What are their positions?

- What are you looking for in terms of a new position? When deciding whether or not to join us, which factors would be most important to you: Compensation? Benefits? Working hours? Opportunities to advance?

SOURCE: *Managing a Small Business Made Easy* by Martin E. Davis (Entrepreneur Press, 2005).

What was the most difficult part of the job? How much teamwork was required? What were the drawbacks of managing a small staff? What were the advantages? General questions such as these will usually yield fairly detailed descriptions.

Then move on to questions designed to reveal personality traits or specific qualities that you consider to be requirements for the job. If you need someone who can deal with stress, ask the candidate to discuss one or two work crises they handled in the past. Note how quickly, directly, and thoroughly the applicant answers.

"Past Behavioral Interviews offer strong evaluative accuracy because the questions they ask *directly* concern the candidates' ability to perform their job."

—Justin Menkes,
author of *Executive Intelligence*

Finally, ask questions to gauge how well the applicant would fit into the company. Try to get a sense of the attitude and work habits the person would bring to your team.

It's critical to find out whether the person you are considering has an employment contract at her current job that puts limitations on future employment, either permanently or for a specified period of time. For example, if the candidate's employer is in a similar business to yours, and her contract has a "no competition" clause, she might be prohibited from working for your company.

Assessing Attitude

Many employers believe that people can be taught skills—but that their character is fixed. Thus, they specifically look for people with the attitude or personality that will mesh with their organization's culture.

To weed out candidates who might have the experience for the job but not the right stuff, a technique called behavior-based interviewing was developed. In this approach, candidates are asked to give examples of how they performed or behaved in the past in specific situations. For example, to assess leadership ability, you might ask, "Can you tell me about a time when you had to persuade someone to do something that he or she did not want to do? What did you say to them and what was the result?" In behavior-based interviews, all questions attempt to elicit examples of how the candidate has handled situations in the past that demonstrate particular desirable qualities.

It's important to get detailed descriptions. If a candidate's first account of his experience is too general or vague, follow up with more questions.

Dos & Don'ts ☑

GETTING THE MOST OUT OF INTERVIEWS
Here are some guidelines for effective interviewing:

☐ Do review all the applicant's paperwork right before the interview.

☐ Do consider beforehand which questions will elicit the facts you need to make a decision.

☐ Do pose the same set of questions to all candidates, in order to make a point-for-point comparison.

☐ Do try to make the candidate feel at ease—by offering water or coffee, for example.

☐ Don't put a desk or physical barrier between you and the candidate.

☐ Do establish a rapport and adopt a relaxed, friendly attitude.

☐ Do make the applicant aware of your position and what you do.

☐ Do give the applicant some background about the company.

☐ Don't give too much information about the job's responsibilities before asking questions about the candidate's skills and previous responsibilities.

☐ Don't ask questions that might lead to answers that legally cannot be considered when hiring.

☐ Do ask open-ended questions to draw out the applicant.

☐ Don't ask "yes" or "no" questions.

☐ Do listen attentively to the candidate's responses so you can ask good follow-up questions.

☐ Don't fill silences with chatter—give the candidate time to think.

☐ Do give the candidate a chance to ask questions.

☐ Don't talk too much or turn the interview into socializing.

☐ Do conclude the interview by asking the candidate, "Is there anything we haven't covered that you'd like to tell us?"

☐ Do tell the applicant what the next steps are in the hiring process and discuss the time frame for follow-up.

Probe for a couple of recent examples of each situation. Look for answers that show that the candidate took responsibility for the outcome.

This technique works well in many situations. The secret is to identify the qualities and behaviors you want in a candidate, and then to formulate questions that will elicit accounts of how candidates have displayed those qualities in the past. Here are a few examples of typically desirable traits in job candidates and the questions or approaches designed to reveal whether someone has demonstrated them:

Outside the Box

TALENT AND VALUES

When hiring new staff members, former Dial Corporation CEO Herb Baum wanted candidates with strong values and character as well as good credentials. Some of the things he looked for were:

- A caring spirit

- Creativity

- Pride in achievement

Competent performers without good characters will eventually fail, according to Baum. "Substance and a strong character determine sustainability," he writes.

SOURCE: *The Transparent Leader* by Herb Baum and Tammy Kling (Collins, 2004).

- If you are looking for someone who's passionate about her work, find out what she likes most about her current job and why. Solicit an example of a time when the candidate was so involved with a project she put everything else aside to work on it. Ask how the candidate has handled a situation when she didn't believe in a project or a mission.
- If you are looking for a person who delivers on commitments, ask how the candidate managed commitments in previous jobs. Who set the direction and made the plans? If there were setbacks, how did she deal with them? To what extent did she achieve her goals?
- If integrity matters, ask the candidate to describe a situation in which her integrity was challenged at work—for instance, a colleague asked her to tell a lie.
- If flexibility is important, ask the candidate to talk about a situation in which she had to change plans to accommodate the needs of a coworker.
- If time management skills are critical, ask the candidate to describe a situation in which she had to prioritize among various demands on her time. How did she decide which task to complete first, second, and third?
- If the ability to innovate is important, have the candidate tell you about a situation in which she had to develop new methods and techniques.
- If you want to know how the candidate deals with obstacles, ask her to tell you how she tackled a particularly challenging goal.

- If the job requires handling customers, ask the candidate how she resolved a recent difficult customer interaction.
- If setting high personal standards is a quality that you desire in a candidate, ask her to describe those she currently holds for herself and to rate the job she's doing in living up to them.

One final note: Be careful of trying to find—or of favoring—candidates whose attitudes and personality match your own. You're not looking for a clone, but rather for someone who will complement you and your workforce.

Outside the Box

PROBING QUESTIONS

Experienced interviewers quickly develop a list of favorite questions, ones they feel yield strong, revealing answers. Mark Jaffe, president of Wyatt & Jaffe in Minneapolis, has a particularly shrewd question he likes to ask job candidates, "What are people's greatest misperceptions about you?" Jaffe finds the answers very enlightening because, as he explains, "What you view as misperceptions are other people's truths."

Dennis Spring, president of Spring Associates in New York, asks, "If I were to call your manager, what would he or she say is the one thing that you're relied on for the most?" Spring recommends

Interviewing Entry-Level Candidates

The basic techniques of interviewing are the same no matter what the position. It's likely, however, that you will spend less time with applicants who are new to the job market—perhaps just half an hour—and that you will spend more time finding out about their personal qualities and character rather than skills and experience. When interviewing college graduates, ask them to tell you about something they've done that they're proud of—such as completing a biking race for charity—or about the question, since "the answer tells me how she perceives herself in the organization, but not through her own eyes."

Jim McSherry, managing partner of McSherry & Associates 2 in Westchester, Illinois, asks job candidates, "If I were to talk with the people who know you best, how would they describe you?" McSherry says applicants almost always offer him an honest self-appraisal, which, coincidentally, "summarizes and confirms what I've learned about them during the time we've been talking."

SOURCE: "Don't Be Blindsided by Recruiters' Questions" by Perri Capell, *CareerJournal.com* (March 29, 2004).

CASE *FILE*

POSITIVE FOCUS

How do you build a capable army when most of your officers have no actual experience leading troops? World War II Army chief of staff George C. Marshall, who was famous for his ability to get the right people into the right job, found a way. When his aides would challenge him, pointing out a weakness in a candidate, Marshall would always ask, "What is the assignment? To train a division? If he is first-rate as a trainer, put him in. The rest is my job." Using this tactic—focusing on what a candidate could do rather than on what he couldn't—Marshall built an army of 13 million men.

SOURCE: *The Daily Drucker* by Peter Drucker (HarperBusiness, 2004).

a recent accomplishment that exceeded their expectations. You will quickly determine whether the applicant is the kind of person who gives 110 percent or the type who merely gets by. In addition, ask about any tasks or projects they've completed that required skills comparable to those that they would need on the job.

Questions You Can't Ask

Certain questions are legally off limits during a job interview, and it's critical to know which ones to stay away from. In general, if a question does not relate directly to the individual's job history or his or her performance of the job, don't ask it.

> "If you hire great people and involve them intensively in the hiring process, you'll get more great people."
>
> —Eric Schmidt,
> CEO of Google

Avoid any questions that could leave you open to a charge of discrimination. Questions about activities, interests, or hobbies may inadvertently open the door to a discussion of religious or political beliefs, which the law forbids during employment interviews. To avoid charges of sexual discrimination, never ask a women about her marital status, her plans to have children, or her child-care or senior-care arrangements. If you're concerned about any of these issues, ask a performance-based question on the subject instead. For instance, if you fear that caring for an ailing parent might cause the candidate to miss work, ask how often she has been absent from her current or past job.

Don't ask questions about any disabilities, about citizenship, about a past history of filing workers' compensation claims, where a person grew up, or when he or she graduated from high school or college.

Red Flags ⚐◆

DISCRIMINATORY QUESTIONS

It pays to become familiar with laws governing hiring practices before starting the interview process so that you know which questions or topics to avoid. Here is a list of some potential troublemakers:

- Are you married?

- What is your spouse's name?

- What is your maiden name?

- Do you have any children?

- Are you pregnant?

- What are your child-care or senior-care arrangements?

- What is your race?

- What is your country of origin?

Be careful not to say anything that a candidate can later use as ammunition. Mike Poskey, vice president of ZERORISK HR, Inc., a Dallas-based human resources risk-management firm, issues the following caution to managers in his about. com article "How to Interview Legally and Effectively": "Avoid making statements during the interview process that could be alleged to create a contract of employment. When describing the job, avoid using terms like 'permanent,' 'career

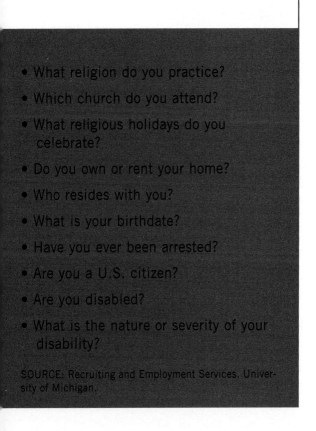

- What religion do you practice?

- Which church do you attend?

- What religious holidays do you celebrate?

- Do you own or rent your home?

- Who resides with you?

- What is your birthdate?

- Have you ever been arrested?

- Are you a U.S. citizen?

- Are you disabled?

- What is the nature or severity of your disability?

SOURCE: Recruiting and Employment Services, University of Michigan.

job opportunity,' or 'long-term.'" Poskey further warns hiring managers not to say anything that might imply job security—or else if the employee is laid off at some point, he might feel he has grounds for a lawsuit.

Types of Interviews

Every company has evolved its own method of conducting job interviews, although interview protocols vary based on the responsibilities of the job to be filled. It's not necessary for all interviews to follow the standard scenario in which the hiring manager sits on one side of his desk and the candidate on the other. If you're looking for candidates who can think outside the box, it might be helpful to interview them outside the box. Nontraditional interviews can also highlight whether the candidate possesses the qualities you're looking for—the ability to roll with new concepts, for instance.

If you want candidates to open up, create an interview forum that's relaxed and casual: sit at a round table, or on the same side of the desk; meet in the company cafeteria, or even outside under a tree. Offer the candidate a soda or coffee, and begin with some light conversation. Make your questions tactful and sensitive, never challenging. When interviewing a potential coworker rather than a potential staff member, this more casual approach may encourage candidates to express themselves freely and reveal their less formal side.

If, on the other hand, you want to measure a candidate's ability to deal with stress, the interview could simulate a high-pressure situation. Try sitting at the opposite end of a conference table or on the other side of a large desk. Start with a series of difficult questions, and don't supply the candidate with positive feedback. Maintain the pressure by following up on every answer with a challenge, forcing the candidate to show her mettle.

"Today, many companies are reporting that their number one constraint on growth is the inability to hire workers with the necessary skills."

—Bill Clinton,
former U.S. president

Few people work in a vacuum, so it's important to discover how candidates deal with groups of people with different personalities. With this in mind, a group interview might be your next step. Gather several people with various personality traits, give each of them your list of questions, and have everyone jump in and fire away. A one-on-one interview may follow, where you can discuss the candidate's reactions to the various staff members.

> "A conversation is the only way to expose and judge the cognitive skills a candidate uses to reach an answer. It is the process that led the person to their conclusion that reveals their strengths and weaknesses."
>
> —Justin Menkes

Documenting the Interview

It's important to take notes during an interview so that you'll have a record of what each candidate said in order to review and discuss it with other interviewers. It's also helpful to write down candidates' actual answers to questions, rather

Plan B

INTERVIEWING AND HIRING AS A TEAM

Most businesses prefer having at least three different people interview a job candidate, so they can base their decision on several opinions. A team approach allows tasks such as screening, formulating effective questions, and checking references to be shared or delegated.

According to Rama Dev Jager and Ortiz Rafael, authors of *In the Company of Giants: Candid Conversations with the Visionaries of the Digital World,* candidates for jobs at Apple Computers talk to at least a dozen people in several areas of the company. When making a final decision, consensus is the goal: a candidate is rejected if even one out of 10 interviewers questions the fit. At Google, candidates talk to half a dozen interviewers, both managers and potential colleagues. At a Microsoft interview, a candidate might spend a day shuttling from office to office on the Redmond campus while the interviewers share their opinions and impressions with each other in e-mails.

than your evaluations or conclusions. At the beginning of the interview, be courteous and let the candidate know that you will be taking notes.

Concluding the Interview

Before the interview is over, make sure to give the applicant a chance to ask questions and to add anything that might be important for you to know in order to make your hiring decision. A candidate who asks thoughtful and knowledgeable questions is demonstrating a high

Red Flags ✕◆

WEEDING OUT PROBLEM CANDIDATES

Recruitment experts say that a standard application is one of the most effective ways to avoid hiring a liar. According to Lester Rosen, attorney and president of Employment Screening Services of Novato, California, "Warning signs include neglecting to sign the application, which could shield the candidate from being accused of falsification, or not consenting to a background check." Also, if the work history portion of the form shows gaps of employment, ask the candidate to clarify.

It's important to follow up with the individual if the application is missing level of interest and motivation—traits that will ultimately benefit your company.

If an applicant is a strong contender, you may also want to give him a brief tour of the office and introduce him to other employees who can answer his questions. It's always a good idea for the candidate to get the "feel" of the space he will be working in.

Finally, tell the applicant about the next steps in the hiring procedure—whether there will be a second interview, for instance. Let candidates

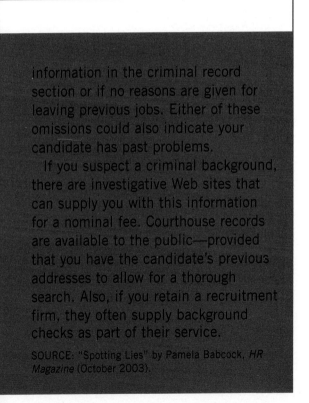

information in the criminal record section or if no reasons are given for leaving previous jobs. Either of these omissions could also indicate your candidate has past problems.

If you suspect a criminal background, there are investigative Web sites that can supply you with this information for a nominal fee. Courthouse records are available to the public—provided that you have the candidate's previous addresses to allow for a thorough search. Also, if you retain a recruitment firm, they often supply background checks as part of their service.

SOURCE: "Spotting Lies" by Pamela Babcock, *HR Magazine* (October 2003).

know that you will be checking their references before coming to a decision. Then give the applicant a rough idea of your time frame for making that decision.

> ## "When in doubt, don't hire—keep looking."
>
> —Jim Collins,
> author of *Good to Great*

Follow-Up Interviews

If you've narrowed down your search to a few strong candidates, you might want them to be interviewed by others in your group. In addition to managers, include peers and subordinates in this process—to eliminate candidates who snub those lower in the pecking order. Be aware that each interviewer will probably view the individual differently, not only because the candidate may demonstrate a different level of energy and preparedness with different people, but because of the interviewers' varying points of view. As a manager, you need to decide which of these reactions are valid and which might be biased.

If you haven't already requested a list of references, end your round of follow-up interviews by asking for the names of former bosses, colleagues, direct reports, and character references. It's important that you contact as many of these people as you can to corroborate information provided in the interviews. If the candidate has not yet signed a release permitting you to question references, this is the time for him to do so. The form should state that the applicant agrees not to sue you or any former employers based on what you learn during the reference checks.

CHECKING OUT PROMISING PROSPECTS

Lies and exaggerations on resumes are increasingly common. A 2004 survey of 2,500 human resource professionals conducted by the Society for Human Resource Management reported that 96 percent of respondents said their companies always check references, credentials, or both. It's becoming easier than ever for an employer to discover the truth, either by hiring a specific outside firm to check the candidate's background and confirm information on his or her resume and application, or by doing their own legwork. A visit to Google or other Internet search sites can yield a wealth of facts on an individual in minutes. In addition, various specialized tests can generate still other information.

Touching Base with Previous Employers

It's critical to check an applicant's references before offering them a job. Never forget that you can now be held liable for a new hire who becomes violent and injures an employee or customer, or who commits fraud, providing it is proven in court that completing a reference check would have kept you from hiring the applicant.

Checking employment references can be tricky, however. In spite of the growing number of states with laws protecting companies that supply good-faith references—called reference check immunity laws—from litigation, many companies still shy away from revealing anything but bare-bones information about a former worker.

Your first step should be getting a candidate's permission to contact his previous employers, especially if he is currently employed. Next, fax a copy of the background-check waiver that the employee signed during the interview to the employer, along with a letter on your company's stationery requesting information on the employee. Follow up with a phone call.

During your call, first verify basic information—employment dates, title, salary, and work performed. Then, based on what the applicant told you about his experience, ask specific questions about his attitude and level of performance. Pay attention if you get lukewarm, neutral, or negative feedback. Ask the former employer if he or she would rehire the candidate and ask for an explanation of the answer, whether positive or negative.

After calling former supervisors, get in touch with other people the candidate worked with—including direct reports and colleagues. If you hear three positive references and one negative, dig a little deeper to make sure that the negative feedback is not from old rival looking to get even.

Checking Candidates' Background and Academic Record

In recent years, it's become common practice to run criminal checks on potential employees—especially since technology has made these checks easier and less expensive to perform.

Behind the Numbers

HOW EMPLOYERS CHECK OUT CANDIDATES

There are numerous sources for finding the truth behind a resume's "smokescreen." Which screening and assessment methods you use often depends on the job at stake. Here are some of the methods companies frequently employ to check for potential problems:

Method	Currently use	Increased use in past 5 years
Any screening	93%	48%
Background checks	79	51
Prescreening programs	57	51
Skills testing	56	48
Behavioral interviewing	54	56
Drug tests	50	54
Behavioral assessments	34	60
Credit checks	33	55

SOURCE: "The Spherion® Emerging Workforce® Study," Spherion Corporation © 2006 Spherion Pacific Enterprises LLC.

In fact, 80 percent of companies surveyed for a 2004 Society for Human Resources Management report said they run a criminal check on applicants. Of 8 million criminal checks run by the data firm ChoicePoint, which provides online and offline services to many large companies, 9 percent turned up felony convictions not disclosed by applicants. Nearly half of those surveyed also check motor vehicle records, and more than half verify education records. An applicant's claim to possess a degree from a particular university can easily be verified with a phone call to the school.

Credit Checks

According to the Society for Human Resource Management report, 35 percent of employers now run credit checks on potential hires, a sizable increase from the 19 percent reported in 1996. Some companies regard credit checks as a fast, efficient way to narrow the range of applicants, since people who earn good credit are assumed to have a strong sense of responsibility. If the credit report is poor, you might want to move on to the next candidate.

Personality Tests

Studies have indicated that assessment or "profile" tests can be a far more reliable predictor of employee performance than interviews and resumes alone. Yet for years these tests remained out of favor after their misuse led to discriminatory complaints and subsequent legislation to restrict them.

Outside the Box

IDENTIFYING "A" PLAYERS

How do you separate the wheat from the chaff during the hiring process? Industrial psychologist Bradford Smart uses a process he calls "topgrading" to weed out underachievers—or C players—and to identify superstars—the top 10 percent of talent available for a particular position in an industry. Smart advises his clients to hire only As and Bs, willing and able workers who can be coached to achieve higher levels. To determine strengths, weaknesses, and job expectations, and thus predict future performance, Smart pores over a candidate's career looking for patterns, asking hundreds of questions covering every job, every success, and every failure. For instance, he asks them about every boss they've had and informs them that all their bosses from the past decade will be contacted—and then he does just that. The A players take it in stride.

SOURCE: *Topgrading* by Bradford Smart (Portfolio, 2005).

Today they are definitely making a comeback; as a hiring tool that can indicate level of performance, and in many cases employee longevity, they are growing in popularity. Larger corporations have been giving assessment tests to applicants for more than a decade, and now smaller companies, schools, and other institutions are also starting to view them as a valuable screening mechanism. Financial advisory firms often use psychometric assessments, personality profiling, and intelligence tests when hiring new employees. Although the concept has generated some controversy, personality testing has become a $400

ASSESSING WITHOUT BREAKING THE LAW

Since the use of personality tests to assess job candidates has become controversial, Joseph Schmitt, a labor attorney at Halleland Lewis Nilan & Johnson in Minneapolis, warns that "Employers need to do their homework before using tests" to determine an applicant's fit for a job. He recommends finding out the answers to the following questions before using a particular test:

Is it in compliance with all current U.S. civil-rights and equal-opportunity legislation?

Has the maker of the test ever been sued?

million industry in the United States.

There are a number of types of tests available that each serve a slightly different function, but they all offer employers a more comprehensive view of a candidate's abilities. In simplistic terms, I.Q. tests measure what you can do, personality tests gauge what you like to do, and psychometric tests determine what you will or won't do.

The most popular tests feature questionnaires that classify candidates into general personality types. The questions in the widely

Has it proven to be an accurate predictor of an employee's future performance in various objective studies?

You might also want to contact your company's legal department to check a particular test's compliance with labor laws. After administering the test, consider hiring an experienced professional, such as an industrial-organizational psychologist, to interpret the results.

SOURCE: "More Employers Are Using Personality Tests as Hiring Tools" by Victoria Knight, *CareerJournal.com* (March 21, 2006).

THE BOTTOM LINE

used Myers-Briggs Type Indicator test measure an individual's traits and tendencies on four scales: introversion and extroversion, sense and intuition, thinking and feeling, judging and perceiving. The test categorizes people according to their combination of traits. For example, those who rate as highly "extroverted, sensing, thinking, and judging" are identified as natural leaders who excel at directing action and organizing projects.

The Minnesota Multiphasic Personality Inventory test is widely used to spot substance abuse and other symptoms of social maladjustment. About 60 percent of U.S. police departments use the test, as do banks and retailers.

These tests can cost as little as $300 per employee, including consultancy fees. Not a bad bargain for something that, if properly used, can cut costs and improve the quality of new hires.

As with interview questions, some tests might be considered unlawful if not specifically designed as a hiring tool. Before administering any tests, check your state laws.

And if it happens that you've nailed down the perfect candidate for your job opening, and he or she flubs the required assessment test, consider the words of Dr. Wendell Williams of scientificselection.com, the guru of corporate psychological testing: "The only test that is truly credible, is one that tests critical aspects of a job, such as driving a car. Such tests are reliable 64% of the time." So bear in mind that assessment tests should be regarded as an indicator for screening purposes, not a foolproof guarantee of talent or ability.

Job Simulations

With hiring costs escalating, employers need more assurance that a candidate can perform in actual work situations. In light of that, applicants are frequently asked to engage in

CASE *FILE*

A DAY IN THE LIFE

It had become common practice for DaimlerChrysler's Chrysler Group to ask hourly wage manufacturing candidates to perform tasks demonstrating their abilities, but the division recently began requiring the tests of plant-manager applicants, as well. These candidates experience a typically stressful "day-in-the-life," including receiving memos and phone calls, and frequent interruptions from "employees" with job problems. Some managers have mixed feelings about the tests, calling them overkill, while others see them as a way to custom-fit the worker to the job.

SOURCE: "Employers Gauge Candidates' Skills at 'Real-World' Tasks" by Erin White, *Wall Street Journal Online* (January 16, 2006).

office simulations. A managerial simulation might include fielding phone calls from suppliers, employee conferences, sending and receiving constant e-mails, and other pressure situations, which allow employers to see first-hand how well a candidate copes. Executive simulations up the ante even further, and can include negotiating a worker conflict or handling difficult questions from a reporter. There is also software available geared to specific jobs: Teller Vision Simulation© replicates banking situations right on the PC.

Simulations are also used to test candidates for blue-collar jobs. Toyota and GM use simulations at certain plants to test applicants on their problem-solving skills, their ability to follow simple instructions, and how they work with a team. At one auto assembly plant, applicants run a simulated business involving the manufacture of circuit boards. Their goal is to come up with ideas and then decide on the best way to find suppliers, assemble the boards, and maintain quality control. Some Toyota candidates are also required to test their manual dexterity and spatial skills; they might spend their "work" day assembling and disassembling a set of plastic pipes.

THE FINAL DECISION

A number of factors enter into a final hiring decision—not only the candidate's experience, qualifications, references, and salary requirements, but also the impressions you and your fellow interviewers have of the candidate's suitability for the position and fit within your group.

Before you make a job offer, it's critical to have a strong sense of having found the right person for the position. You and your company will be making a significant investment of time and money in this individual, and you want it to pay off.

WELCOME
ABOARD

> "I am convinced that nothing we do is more important than hiring and developing people. At the end of the day, you bet on people, not on strategies."

—Larry Bossidy,
author of *Execution*

You've narrowed down your candidate database, created a short-list, interviewed the most promising prospects, invited them back for follow-up meetings, discussed all the possibilities with your team, decided on an employee, and checked his or her references.

Now, it's time to make the offer and welcome your new team member. The conversations you have during the hiring period and decisions you subsequently make set in motion a cycle of goal setting and performance management that will help keep your new employee motivated and growing and making positive contributions to your business for years to come.

CRAFTING YOUR OFFER

Before you actually contact the candidate to make an official offer, you need to nail down the issues of salary, bonuses, benefits, and any other perks you are considering.

Salary

The first decision you need to make is the salary you intend to offer. If you have access to information on industry salary standards, you are in a good position to set a salary that is fair for the individual's background, talent, experience, and salary history. To research what other companies are paying, survey classified ads or consult professional and trade associations, human resources specialists, and recruiters in your field. Websites such as www.wetfeet.com, www.salary.com, and www.jobstar.org offer a great deal of pertinent information.

Many companies set salary grades or ranges for each type of position, expecting the hiring manager to negotiate within that given range. The grades may be narrow and specific (e.g., $25,000–$32,000 for entry-level analysts), or fairly broad, based on an individual's knowledge, skills, and experience in comparison with others in the same job. Not all salaries are straight salaries, however.

> "As an acid test of hiring, ask yourself how you would feel having the candidate working for your competition instead of you."
>
> — Harvey B. Mackay,
> author of *Swim with the Sharks Without Being Eaten Alive*

Some individuals, often those working in sales, are paid using a performance-based system that links compensation to accomplishments—for example, an employee making $36,000 a year could potentially increase his income to $40,000 by meeting designated goals, such as decreasing outsourcing or raising productivity. The extra $4,000 would be paid as a yearly bonus, and the base salary would remain $36,000 for the next year. If these objectives aren't reached, the employee's pay rate does not rise above the base wage or salary. Performance-based pay systems have been shown to make employees more effective and productive than straight salaries. A 2006 survey by WorldatWork, an association for human resources professionals, showed that 79 percent of employers now use performance-based pay, up from 66 percent in 2001.

Some employers use a skill-based system, basing pay on the number of skills the employee possesses. More than half of all Fortune 500 companies reward at least some of their workers on this basis, usually those in the manufacturing sector. When employees acquire new skills, their pay increases, and if each skill is assigned a price according to its value to the business, employees are motivated to acquire new skills. Some employers also add the incentive of a variable-pay program and give bonuses for extraordinary individual or group performance in addition to skill-based pay.

Whatever your system is, it's important that you explain it to the prospective employee when you present your offer. Also tell your chosen candidate how his or her work will be evaluated, how superior performance will be rewarded, and what measures you use to determine incentive payouts, if any.

Bonuses

In addition to offering a powerful performance incentive to employees, bonuses benefit corporations by allowing them to reward key players without raising their fixed costs.

During the hiring process, you will quickly learn that bonuses can also be a major component in salary negotiations. For this reason, you need to be aware of the various types of bonuses your company offers.

Annual bonuses are given each year to all eligible employees. The amount varies from year to year depending on what the company has earned and how the individual employees who are being rewarded have performed.

Though annual bonuses are typically paid in a single sum at the end of the year, other types of bonuses can be used as incentives and rewards at various times.

Signing bonuses are offered as incentives for the most desirable candidates to sign on with a firm, especially in fields that are intensely competitive. (The employee has to remain with the company for a specified period of time, however, or repay the bonus.)

Incentive bonuses are given (to both individuals and groups) to reward an important accomplishment or outstanding performance, such as a payment to an advertising agency's design team when their campaign wins a major new client.

Retention bonuses are given to attempt to keep especially valuable employees, such as specialists or high-performing managers and executives, from leaving.

If your salary offer is less than stellar, consider sweetening the pot with a bonus—either now or in the future—to win over a candidate who may be wavering.

Outside the Box

ALTERNATIVES TO STRAIGHT SALARY

Traditional salaries are what most employees are familiar with. That standard is changing, however, as more companies begin to offer alternative types of salaries. These newer models are based on incentives or skills and are intended to align an employee's pay with the effort he puts into his job—and the degree to which those efforts impact the bottom line.

The Variable Pay Model – Variable pay, or "pay at risk" is contingent upon performance or generated results. It is a way of "incentivizing" employees and then allowing them to share in the profit from their increased contributions to productivity. When companies offer these incentives, employees are less likely to leave, good performers feel rewarded, and the companies aren't as likely to have to downsize due to high overhead.

The Skill-Based Model – Many companies are now compensating employees for certain work-related skills they acquire, or for being able to perform additional or more technical tasks. Once the employee has demonstrated a satisfactory level of competence, their base pay is increased.

Used since the 1940s on assembly lines, when one worker had to step in for another, skill-based pay has recently been revived as downsized businesses attempt to cross-train workers.

The Share-and-Share-Alike Model – The ESO or employee share ownership plan is still something of a revolutionary notion, even though it came to light over 200 years ago in a Scottish industrial town. The premise of the plan is that all workers are partners in a concern. By turning employees into shareholders, a company increases their emotional investment in their daily work—and in the overall success of the organization. At certain firms, employees are encouraged to save a portion of their salaries, and then, at the end of a set time period, allowed to use the money to buy company shares at a discount. This type of plan, in which compensation is offered for measurable improvements, can also have an impact on safety and attendance records.

SOURCE: "Variable Pay Programs Provide Flexibility, Incentives" by Joan Lloyd, Joanlloyd.com (February 4, 1996); "Skill Based Pay: A Brief Overview" Effectivecompensation.com (2003).

Benefits

A first-class benefits plan will make your company attractive to both top managers and the most skilled hourly wage earners. So before delivering your offer, make sure you know the specifics of your company's benefits plan and mentally highlight its strong points. Then talk up its positive points and don't mention what might be missing.

The most attractive health care plans are those that minimize a worker's out-of-pocket contribution. Some large companies cover only about 80 percent of the cost of medical insurance for employees and their dependents, while smaller companies may cover all health insurance costs for employees, but not cover their spouses and dependents. Short-term disability coverage can be a selling point, since not all employers offer it, although many provide life and long-term disability insurance. Stock options or stock grants can provide long-term incentives to employees and can help keep valuable employees from leaving during a firm's start-up phase.

There are also nontraditional benefits companies offer that make life easier and more efficient for employees. During your hiring interview, don't forget to spotlight such benefits as onsite gyms, laundry rooms, massage rooms, hair cuts, car washes, dry cleaning services, dining facilities, commuting buses, concierge service, backup child- and adult-care services, half-day Fridays or permanent four-day holiday weekends.

If your firm offers other perks or programs—employee assistance programs (which covers everything from substance abuse programs to psychological counseling to legal assistance), discounts on company products, or the use of company cars—be sure to mention it to your candidate.

EMPLOYEE LEAVE AND THE LAW
Under the Family and Medical Leave Act of 1993, certain employers must give eligible employees up to 12 work weeks of unpaid leave during any 12 months for the birth and care of a newborn child, an adoptee, or a foster child; for the care of a spouse, child or parent with a serious health condition; and when the employee is unable to work because of a serious health condition.

The law typically covers employers with 50 or more employees and applies to workers who have been employed by the company for at least 12 months and have worked at least 1,250 hours during the 12 months before the leave starts.

SOURCE: "The Family and Medical Leave Act of 1993," U.S. Department of Labor Fact Sheet No. 28, dol.gov. (December 5, 2006).

THE BOTTOM LINE

The Pension Plan

As more and more U.S. companies are forced to focus on the bottom line, pension plans are coming under fire. Many organizations are switching to 401(k) plans, which are less expensive than traditional pension plans. As a hiring manager,

> "It is easy to be penny wise and pound foolish with respect to benefits that can save employees considerable time and improve their health and productivity."
>
> — Sergey Brin and Larry Page, founders of Google

you need to be aware of what's out there and understand how your plan compares to others. You will also need to be able to explain your company's pension plan to job candidates. In fact, if your program is a good one, you'll want to make a point of emphasizing its strengths when highlighting company benefits to a strong job contender.

There are three basic types of pension plans: traditional pension plans, which are broken into two categories, "qualified" or "nonqualified," and the new cash-balance plans, signed into law by President George W. Bush in August 2006.

Qualified pension plans. With a traditional pension, when employees retire, they typically receive a monthly payment for the rest of their life. Employer contributions are tax-deductible, and inside the plan, the money grows tax-free since employee contributions are not taxable until the funds are distributed, which is usually at retirement age, when employees are likely in a lower tax bracket. Qualified pension plans fall into two categories—defined benefit plans and defined contribution plans—both governed by legislation.

In a defined benefit plan, retired employees receive a fixed amount, based on age, salary, and number of years with the company. The amount of the benefit grows slowly at first, then rises sharply as the worker ages, earns more money, and puts in more years with the company. While defined benefit plans formerly covered roughly 40 percent of the work force, today they cover less than 20 percent.

Employees contribute to their pension accounts in a defined plan, therefore assuming a share of the investment risk. Some employers also contribute to defined plans, usually by matching some or all of the employee's contribution. A 401(k) is a defined contribution plan.

Nonqualified pension plans. Nonqualified plans are designed to provide deferred compensation for executives and high-level employees. These plans don't earn the tax breaks available for qualified plans, however, and the company's payments into the plan are not income tax-deferred until the actual compensation has been paid out, which could be years away. The famous "golden parachute," in which senior or key employees are promised compensation in excess of their salaries if control of the corporation changes, is a nonqualified pension plan. Another variation is the "golden handcuff," where employees earn supplemental retirement benefits by remaining with a company for a specific amount of time or until reaching a certain age.

Cash-balance plans. The recent federal legislation is expected to encourage more companies to shift to cash-balance plans, a hybrid that combines features of both traditional pension and 401(k) plans. Each year an employer contributes a certain percentage of an employee's salary to an account, and guarantees that the account will grow annually by a fixed amount or at a variable rate tied to a financial benchmark, for instance, one-year Treasury Bills. Employers are responsible for investing the funds in a cash-balance plan, which is federally insured against loss. When workers leave the company or retire, they can take the balance in a lump payment and roll it over into an Individual Retirement Account or they can choose an annuity that provides a guaranteed monthly income for the rest of their lives. Supporters of cash-balance plans insist they make the most sense, especially in the current job climate, where few people stay with one company long enough to accrue a traditional pension.

Time Off

It's important to review time-off benefits with your candidate. Even office superstars need a restorative break, so emphasize that your company understands this. Employers commonly allow time off for major holidays, sick days, personal days, and vacations. Some offer employees a set number of days off each year rather than distinguishing between sick, vacation, and personal days. Some employers offer a "floating holiday," which allows employees time off for religious observances not covered in the annual schedule. Some American companies have started following the European model, allowing four or even five weeks of vacation, but one or two weeks is typical. Tell your candidate at what point in the calendar year he can begin taking vacation time, and when the number of weeks will increase, say, three weeks vacation after five years with the company. Also discuss whether vacation time can be carried over from one year to the next.

Remember, a generous vacation policy makes a good job offer even more appealing—and may even compensate for a slightly smaller salary.

Flexible Schedules

If your salary offer isn't quite up to par, you might still persuade a candidate to take the job by offering more time off or flexible work hours. As Jill Hamburg Coplan reported in "Making the Case for Telecommuting" in *BusinessWeek Online*, a recent survey by online benefits company LifeCare found that flexible work arrangements were the most coveted employee benefit, even more desirable than healthcare. Telecommuting or working from home has surged in recent years, especially in high-tech companies. Research indicates that allowing employees to telecommute reduces absenteeism and turnover, improves productivity, and

SMALL COMPANY PERKS

If you work for a smaller company and feel that you can't compete with larger firms and their higher salaries and rich benefits packages, don't sell yourself short when making an offer. While it's true that salaries might not be as competitive, many smaller firms compensate with on-the-job perks and other benefits, such as:

- The opportunity to be more hands-on

- The need to wear multiple hats, which results in wider experience and enhanced skills

- More chances for recognition

increases levels of satisfaction. Some employers even report that telecommuting can benefit
the bottom line. One example is Development
Counselors International, a New York City–based
economic-analysis firm, which saw its western
business triple when two 15-year veterans began
telecommuting from the West Coast.

Balancing All Factors

In areas or industries where the pool of job candidates is limited or highly competitive, you may end
up having to sell an applicant on your company.

- The "big frog, small pond" factor,
  which can often result in speedier
  promotions.

- A stronger sense of ownership

- A culture more geared to fulfilling
  employee needs

- Jobs that better utilize an employee's
  aptitudes and interests

- Flextime and telecommuting

- The chance to buy stock options and
  benefit financially from contributions
  to the firm

SOURCE: "Why Small Businesses Pay Less" Salary.com
(2006).

THE BOTTOM LINE

Take a realistic look at the offer you're making and decide if it is fair, competitive, and comprehensive. If you did your homework at the beginning of the search process, you know approximately what this employee is worth in the marketplace, you've researched what other companies are offering, and you know what benefits your company can provide. You are now armed to negotiate.

First, don't immediately assume that any aspects of the job that you yourself see as negative—perhaps the size of the company, limitations of the benefits, or the nature of the work itself—will make the position unappealing to your chosen candidate. No two people have the same set of interests and priorities.

Although some candidates prefer a large corporation that can pay more and provide more benefits, others would rather be at a smaller company where the opportunities are greater. Some individuals are looking for a chance to move up the corporate ladder; others are not as concerned about advancement. Some candidates like variety; others prefer repetitive work.

When you have found a candidate who seems a good fit, someone with the skills and experience needed for the job who seems enthusiastic about the opportunity, make your best offer, reiterate all the benefits, and trust that the candidate will also feel that your company is the right choice.

MAKING THE OFFER

Once you've reached a hiring decision, make the offer as quickly as possible so that you don't lose

Outside the Box

COMPANIES WITH A CONSCIENCE

If you work for a smaller company, and feel that you can't compete with larger firms and their rich benefits packages, don't sell yourself short when making an offer. Small firms have other, less visible advantages. Daniel Solomons, president of the recruiting firm Hyrian, points out that at many small companies employees have more opportunity to interact directly with those at the top and to have a significant impact on the company's direction. Small companies may also be able to provide a casual atmosphere, flexible work schedules, telecommuting opportunities, and other policies that may not be available at large corporations.

Most surveys today reveal that employees want meaningful work, effective coworkers, and recognition for accomplishments on the job; young people are particularly motivated by a company's environmental and community values. If your company stands out in any of these areas, showcase this information in your hiring process.

SOURCE: "Small Business Secrets to Hiring" by Karen E. Klein, *BusinessWeek Online* (August 14, 2006).

your candidate to another employer. You can either make the offer over the phone or in person, but you might prefer a face-to-face meeting so that you can explain all aspects of the salary and benefits package and field any questions from your new hire.

Either way, after stating the title and salary being offered for the position, express your enthusiasm for the candidate and underscore your team's positive response to him or her. Then review the key elements of the job and clarify any special considerations negotiated during the interview process—such as allowing flextime—and outline the benefits package. Then discuss a possible starting date. This is also the time to mention whether your offer is contingent on any conditions—the candidate passing a drug test, medical examination, or criminal records check; providing proof of citizenship or eligibility to work in the country; providing copies of current employment contracts showing post-employment restrictions that could relate to a new job; or completing a probationary period.

It is customary to follow your offer interview with a letter that puts all this information in writing. Also, make sure the letter covers how much notice you will give if the candidate is not successful at the end of the probationary period, if applicable. Most companies ask the candidate to sign the letter and return a copy to the hiring manager.

If the original letter contained pre-hire conditions, send another offer letter without the conditions after the employee has met them.

If a candidate cannot meet the conditions, you are free to withdraw your offer—and you must do this in writing. If the employee starts work before the conditions have been met, make it clear that the offer may be withdrawn if the candidate fails to meet them—for example, if a background check shows that the candidate has lied about a criminal record.

"To get the most out of the people you manage, you must put them in the right spot at the right time."

—Joe Torre,
manager of the New York Yankees

If there is a probationary period and the employee has not developed the skills you expected or is not working out for some other reason, you can withdraw the offer at the end of that period, giving the employee the notice already specified in your offer letter. If no time was specified, give the employee the minimum period of notice accepted in your industry.

If a job candidate is reluctant to accept an offer, find out the reasons why, and try to reach some accord. On the other hand, don't over-negotiate. If you offer a salary that's too far out of line with what others are paid for similar work, your overall compensation scale could suffer. In general, don't bend over backward to persuade a candidate who is not eager to join you. If he does accept under pressure, he may

The BIG Picture

OBLIGATIONS TO AN EMPLOYER

Employees are expected to show loyalty to their employer, even if they do not have a written contract stating their obligations. For those in higher positions, the expectation is for an even greater degree of loyalty. As a hiring manager, you don't want to encourage any breaches of loyalty in job candidates, such as:

- Competing with employer: Although employees may legally make future plans to compete with their employer; while still employed at that company, they may not actually compete.

- Conspiring to compete as a group: Employees cannot intentionally induce others to join them with the intent have second thoughts once he's in place, and you might end up with a whiner instead of a winner.

As soon as you have filled the open position, immediately contact the serious contenders who were not chosen. Let them know you'll be keeping their material on file in case similar positions open up in the future—and make sure you do it. Federal law mandates that all such materials be kept for at least one year after a position is filled. You will also benefit, since it provides you with a pool of screened candidates at the ready.

of undermining or destroying their employer's business.

- Disclosing confidential information: Employees who are privy to confidential information, "trade secrets," or other guarded material on the job may not use or disclose it to outsiders.

- Diverting business opportunites: After giving notice, employees cannot divert potential business away from their current employer. They must continue to pursue business opportunities that benefit their employer until they actually leave the company.

SOURCE: "Strings Attached" by Jonathan A. Segal, *Human Resources* (February 2005).

Next, gather the resume, job application, and your notes on the candidate who got the job and create a personnel file for him. Bear in mind that you must keep this material for three years according to federal law.

Avoid Litigation Over Confidential Information

Hiring candidates who are currently employed can be tricky, since they still owe a certain loyalty to the company they are leaving. To avoid being drawn into litigation, make it clear to applicants that you expect them to honor their obligations. If your new employee has access to confidential information and relationships with customers in her current job, you may want to make a list of actions to be avoided and send it to her.

"Effective organizations put people in jobs in which they can do the most good. They place people—and allow people to place themselves—according to their strengths."

—Peter Drucker

GETTING OFF TO A GOOD START

Getting an employee established in a new job could take some time on your part, but it is time well spent. A worker who feels comfortable and welcome will be motivated and productive.

Many large companies offer orientation sessions at the corporate level if not always at the departmental level. If your business does, so much the better. Still, every job is unique, and you need to anticipate the information, facilities, and services that your new employee will need during his first weeks on the job.

Take care of basics as soon as possible. Make the arrangements necessary for setting up and furnishing an office, cubicle, or desk or other workspace. In large companies, this may mean contacting other departments to line up a computer, e-mail account, phone, and office keys.

Beyond that, new-employee orientation has three facets: familiarizing the employee with corporate policies and procedures; showing him around your office and making introductions, as well as familiarizing him with your building and your neighborhood, so that he knows where to find local services; and getting him started on the job.

The Official Line

During a formal orientation, make sure the employee knows about all company policies and procedures.

Begin by reviewing working hours—starting time, quitting time, and how much time is customary for lunch or breaks. Explain how to keep track of hours worked, if that's necessary in your business. If the employee is eligible for overtime, discuss the rules. Does your department or company offer "comp time" to salaried people who work long hours or take work home?

Tell the employee what the paycheck schedule is. Ask them to complete a 1099 form for withholding of taxes. Discuss policies and procedures relating to bonuses and raises. What can the new employee expect and when?

Familiarize the employee with the benefits program. Sign her up for insurance coverage. Give her written material explaining retirement-plans and other options.

Discuss your policy on vacation, personal days, and days off for religious observances. Let the employee know how to request time off. Is a written request necessary? How far in advance? What happens if the employee doesn't take all vacation time allotted? Some businesses allow vacation pay to accrue (and when you leave a job in California, Illinois, Massachusetts, North Carolina, and Tennessee, you must be offered accrued vacation pay).

Review policies on the use of company property and technology, including e-mail, laptop computers, and the Internet. Discuss ethical issues such as policies on giving and receiving gifts from customers and suppliers.

Go over the company's safety programs, including regulations pertaining to OSHA (the Occupational Safety and Health Administration), fire escape routes, and strategies for getting to work in bad weather.

Outside the Box

IMPROVING YOUR RECRUITING PROCESS

To help you do a better job finding your next great employee, spend some time with your new hire discussing what you did right—and wrong—this time around.

Ask how your new employee found out about the job. If it was through an ad, ask why the ad caught her eye. Find out what worked and didn't work in the hiring process—which parts went smoothly and which made her uncomfortable about the company. Ask about the interviews—were they interesting, provocative, motivational? Did they help the candidate learn about the company? Which parts of the interviewing process were less positive? Did she have other job offers? What was better about their offer? Why did she accept yours? This is also a good time to leverage your new employee's enthusiasm to continue building your network of candidates. Ask for referrals and contact information.

Some companies combine these questions in a questionnaire and ask every new employee to fill it out.

Cover your policy on smoking on the premises. If your building restricts the use of personal fans, electric heaters, lamps, extension cords, or the like, say so.

> "General Electric doesn't have one culture nor does Office Depot or any other company. They have as many cultures as they do managers. People join companies, but they quit their boss."
>
> —Marcus Buckingham,
> author of *First, Break All the Rules* and
> *Now, Discover Your Strengths*

The Settling-In Process

Take your new employee around the office and make introductions. To help her get to know her colleagues, it may be helpful if you ask someone who doesn't already know her to do this.

Give her a departmental phone list and point out the key people she'll need to contact. Show her the photocopying and fax facilities, the supply cabinet, restrooms, ATMs, the company cafeteria or lunchroom, the company library, the vending machines, and explain parking protocol and the corporate Intranet.

Remember that new employees can waste a lot of time searching for information if they aren't told where to find it at the beginning. Anticipate what they will need, and cover it in your orientation tour.

Are there features in the neighborhood that are helpful to know about? Of two neighboring Chinese restaurants, which one is the best? Is there a bistro with a particularly great lunch special? What is the parking situation? If she is using mass transit, point out the location of bus stops or subway stations. Share as much information as you can to help get your new colleague settled.

Starting the Performance Management Cycle

As you begin to put your new hire to work, it's helpful to review the company's business outlook, including its objectives and plans for achieving them. Go over corporate values, product information, competitive position, marketing strategy, manufacturing or service process, and personnel organization.

Next, explain his duties and get him started on an assignment. Make sure he knows exactly what's expected of him and when he is supposed to deliver it.

One of the main reasons some employees fail is that they are not clearly told what is expected of them or given clear goals for the first six months or the first year. So, as you hand over your new employee's first assignment, take the time to spell out performance objectives—this might be "increase the close rate by 15 percent during the next year" or "identify system problems during the next three months." Then set up a schedule—say, every month—to do a formal check on how the new employee is progressing

CASE *FILE*

HOLD ONTO EMPLOYEES BY LETTING THEM GROW

Supermarkets are rarely emblems of upward mobility or high morale, not when you consider the low pay and long hours. Annual turnover in some chains approaches 100% for part-timers and 19% for full-timers, which makes for constant hiring and training.

It's different at Wegmans, a regional supermarket chain that has repeatedly made the list of Fortune's 100 Best Companies to Work For. There, although corporate generosity boosts labor costs to between 15 and 17 percent of sales (compared to 12 percent in other chains), wages and salaries are at the toward these objectives. In between formal visits, stop by periodically to check in. Ask how things are going and probe for specific details that will let you know that your new colleague is on track. If you sense that something is amiss, ask more questions and give feedback. Then be sure to follow up until you are assured that things are going well. Get into the habit of briefly documenting every such conversation with your staff.

RETAINING EMPLOYEES

With skilled workers in such short supply, and given the cost of hiring and training new

high end. Turnover rates hover at about 6 percent, and 20 percent of employees have 10 years of service or more. One secret to Wegmans' success might be their dedication to creating new employment opportunities. Rather than hiring experienced truck drivers to service a new distribution center, Wegmans invited employees to apply for the job. Five months later, Wegmans had enabled two dozen produce clerks and cashiers to become skilled drivers with commercial licenses—and kept valuable employees within the company ranks.

SOURCE: "The Wegmans Way" by Matthew Boyle, *Fortune* (January 2005).

employees, many employers are realizing that it's cost effective to keep their current workforce happy. When you initiate a performance management cycle with a new employee, you are taking an important step toward that goal. By providing frequent on-the-job feedback, you not

THE HIGH COST OF REPLACEMENT

There's a sound financial logic behind keeping workers content—if an employee decides to leave, replacing him could end up costing his company two and a half times his salary. This startling ratio was released in a 2006 survey of 444 North American organizations conducted by Right Management Consultants, the worldwide leader in career transition and organizational consulting. Yet the amount makes sense if you consider the expense of hiring, training, and severance, plus lost productivity while the position remains vacant. In fact, 43 percent of organizations responding said replacing a worker costs at least three times the employee's salary.

SOURCE: "Survey Reveals Top 5 Mistakes Companies Make When Hiring or Promoting," Right Management (June 12, 2006).

THE BOTTOM LINE

only build a relationship with your staff member, you help him grow in his job.

Those two things alone are often enough to keep motivation high. In survey after survey, employees complain that lack of feedback is one of their biggest problems on the job. According to a 2006 Employee Review by Randstad, the world's fourth-largest staffing organization, 86 percent of surveyed workers said they needed to feel valued by their boss to stay happy—but only 37 percent report receiving positive feedback.

So, while it's important not to let your performance management slide, take the time to learn what's important to your new employee—especially her long- and short-term career goals and her expectations regarding her job responsibilities. Show an interest in her family and hobbies. Ask for her ideas about the business. Give her ways to earn time off, and reward her for jobs well done.

Differentiated compensation schemes—better raises—are one way to recognize top performers. At the same time, don't lose sight of your mid-level workers, whose loyalty and effort support your company. According to Harvard Business School professor Thomas J. DeLong, in "Let's Hear It for B Players," *Harvard Business Review* (June 2003), if you ignore workers of this type long enough, they begin to see themselves as low performers. So whenever you can, dig into your corporate pockets, as Procter & Gamble did when it gave every worker a one-time bonus of two extra days of vacation (or the equivalent in cash) in the spring of 2004.

For jobs where a high turnover rate is hard to avoid, specifically repetitive, high-stress jobs such as answering phones at a call center, try to hire people temperamentally suited to the position—friendly, not easily bored by routine, and satisfied by a structured environment and the chance to help others.

Make sure that you show appreciation for these employees' efforts. Pay a little better than you have to, and offer flexible schedules and incentives for specific performance goals. If possible, offer opportunities for advancement to those who successfully spend a predetermined amount of time in the job. Most important, understand your employees' goals in life and do what you can to help them get there.

WHEN IT DOESN'T WORK OUT

Sometimes you can do everything right in the hiring process and still end up with someone who is not a good fit for the job. When that happens, it's best to end the relationship as quickly as possible. Supporting an employee who doesn't have the skills, experience, or motivation to do a job is unfair to the employees who do, plus it becomes a drain on the organization.

Because hiring is so time-consuming, however, it's worth trying to preserve the relationship if some coaching on your part can save it. So if an employee is unaware that there is a problem, point it out without delay.

Work up a plan with the person and indicate you want to see improvement within a reasonable, but limited, time period—say, two weeks.

Be very clear about the improvements you want to see. It is important to immediately document your conversations with notes and put a date on them. Keep them in the employee's file. Careful documentation could be critical if the employee is eventually terminated and sues over the firing.

"The most expensive employee you'll ever hire is the one you have to fire."

—Mel Kleinman,
author of *Hire Tough, Manage Easy*

If the situation does not get better, issue a final warning specifying a brief period in which the employee must improve (e.g., a week). Describe what you require again and explain how your directives have not been met. Ask if there is a problem the employee is not revealing, and offer to work together to resolve it. If the employee's work still does not improve, you will know that you've done all you can.

Deliver the news of termination calmly, objectively, and in private. Because you will have been providing feedback to the employee during the previous three weeks, she will probably not be surprised. It's always wise to have a representative from your company's human resources department present. Show compassion but be firm. Your objective is to make it clear that the decision is final while respecting the employee's dignity.

Improving the Hiring Process

In the scramble to hire and retain talent, managers need all the help they can get. To discover what you're doing right and understand what you could do better, one great tool is the exit interview. That final conversation with human resources in which departing employees speak truthfully about their experiences with the company is a source of valuable information. (In fact, some companies conduct two exit interviews— one on the final day, the other six months later, when employees have a little more distance from the job and feel freer to open up.)

Their frank remarks can guide you as you hire and train their replacements. You may want to ask how the departing employee found his new job—specifically, whether he was recruited or had been actively looking. In addition, ask:

- What he liked and didn't like about his job
- What specific skills he felt were needed for the job
- Whether his work was fulfilling
- What the company could have done to make it more so

- How satisfied he was with the compensation, benefits, and learning opportunities offered
- How he felt about his supervisors and colleagues
- What problems he thinks the company needs to address
- Whether he would consider returning to the company in the future

Hiring the Best Helps Your Bottom Line

Any warm body can fill a chair, but why settle for mediocrity? Just as you use mahogany—not pine—to make fine furniture, a company is only as good as its employees. Having top-notch employees will boost your organization's ability to reach its goals; a high-functioning staff will make your workplace attractive to clients and the general public, including prospective future employees. Having a great work environment with superior workers will help decrease employee turnover and increases efficiency, giving your company the leg-up in the competitive market that it deserves.

Off and Running >>>

You are now ready to put what you have learned from this book into practice. Use this section as a review guide.

CHAPTER 1.
STAR SEARCH: ATTRACTING TOP PERFORMERS

- Mix it up: A diverse workforce can benefit your company with the competitive edge that comes when diverse approaches to problems are tried.

- Do your homework: You won't know what the most important qualities of an employee are until you've sat down and reworked the job description to meet your needs.

- Hire from within: Hiring from within helps cut down on turnover and shows your employees that opportunity for growth is available.

- Advertise where your ideal candidate might be looking: The majority of college grads or those with higher incomes search the Internet for jobs; consider niche job sites for specialized industries.

- Consider candidates who might have the right interests even though they do not possess the ideal experience: Focusing on a candidate's qualities and skills rather than practical experience might serve you better in the long run.

- Build a referral network: Friends of employees and former employees or interns provide a strong field of excellent candidates.

- Make three piles: When reviewing resumes, make a pile each for "yes" (must interview), "no" (not interested), and "maybe." This enables you to get through them quickly.

CHAPTER 2.
INTERVIEWING

- It's okay to prescreen: A telephone interview can help you determine whether or not to ask the candidate in for a face-to-face meeting.

- Don't wing it: Plan your interview so that it goes smoothly.

Off and Running >>>

- Keep your questions open-ended: Let the candidate do most of the talking.

- Find out about contractual obligations: The ideal candidate is going to do you no good if she comes with a noncompetition clause that prevents her from coming to work for you.

- Don't turn an interview into a social call: While interaction should be pleasant, stay on topic and focus on the candidate's capacity and capabilities.

- Take notes: After a while, it's hard to remember which candidate said what; feel free to mark up and make notations on the person's resume.

- Ask the candidate if she has questions: Find out if your prospect asks smart things.

- Don't make a snap decision: Choose your finalists and have somebody else in your company also interview them.

CHAPTER 3.
WELCOME ABOARD

- Decide what salary and other compensation you can offer: Consider a performance-based bonus, profit sharing, or stock options in lieu of an initial salary hike.

- Ensure your candidate is committed to staying: Replacing employees can be expensive.

- Make the offer sooner rather than later: You don't want your candidate to be snatched up by another employer.

- Find out what worked and didn't work in your hiring process: Ask your new employee what caught her eye and appealed to her and what, if anything, made her hesitate.

- Strive for excellence: Set goals and set up a schedule for attaining these goals.

- Allowing your employee upward mobility is a win-win situation: You get a loyal and skilled employee who is satisfied with her job.

Sources

"2006 Recruiting Trends Survey," Direct Employers/Booz Allen Hamilton (January 2006).

Swim with the Sharks without Being Eaten Alive (Reissue edition) by Harvey B. Mackay (Collins, 2005).

"Being the Boss" by Karen Springer, *Newsweek.com* (August 5, 2005).

Winning by Jack Welch (Collins, 2005).

"The Fork in the Road" by Jenny Anderson, *New York Times* (August 6, 2006).

"Changing Top Down Culture Among Managers in Asia" by Cris Prystay, *CareerJournal.com* (May 30, 2006).

"MySQL: Workers in 25 Countries with No HQ" by Josh Hyatt, *Fortune* (June 2006).

"Help Wanted Ads" by Larry Swisher, *BNA Daily Labor Report* (November 8, 2006).

"Paperless Route for Recruiting" by Fay Hanson, *Workforce.com* (February 27, 2006).

"8 Ways to Get the Media Buzzing: Top Strategies for Getting Big Press for Your Small Business" by Mark Nowlan, Entrepreneur.com (July 2006).

"Agencies Warm to Share in Savings" by Gail Repsher Emery, *Washington Technology* (June 2004).

"Keeping in Touch" by Kate O'Sullivan, *CFO Magazine* (December 2005).

It's Not the Big That Eat the Small . . . It's the Fast That Eat the Slow by Jason Jennings and Laurence Haughton (HarperBusiness, 2002).

"Improving Your Employee Referral Program and Justifying Your Investment" by Dave Lefkow, Ere.net (February 21, 2002).

"What's Wrong with Employee Referral Programs?" by Peter D. Weddle, *CareerJournal.com* (September 19, 2005).

"Detroit Forum: Motor City Likes Veterans" by Eilene Zimmerman, *New York Times* (June 18, 2006).

"They Love It Here, and Here and Here," *BusinessWeek Online* (June 4, 2006).

"Student Employment and Job Placement: Tips for Recruiters," Cabrillo College. www.cabrillo.edu

"Recruiters Are Using Games to Assess MBAs" by Ronald Alsop, *Wall Street Journal Online* (August 8, 2006).

"As Talent War Resumes, Recruiters Jump Hoops to Earn Their Fees" by Perri Capell, *Career-Journal.com* (May 3, 2005).

"Spotting Lies" by Pamela Babcock, *HR Magazine* (October 2003).

"Star Search" by Nanette Bymes with Amy Barrett, *Business Week* (October 10, 2005).

"The Spherion® Workforce® Study," reprinted with permission from Spherion Corporation. ©2006 Spherion Pacific Enterprises LLC.

In Search of Excellence by Thomas J. Peters and Robert H. Waterman, Jr. (HarperCollins, 1986)

Managing for Dummies by Bob Nelson and Peter Economy (Wiley, 2003).

"To Hire Sharp Employees, Recruit in Sharp Ways" by William C. Taylor, *New York Times* (April 23, 2006).

The Transparent Leader by Herb Baum and Tammy King (Collins, 2004).

Managing a Small Business Made Easy by Martin E. Davis (Entrepreneur Press, 2005).

The Daily Drucker by Peter Drucker (HarperBusiness, 2004).

"How to Interview Legally and Effectively" by Mike Poskey, about.com, n.d.

Recruiting and Employment Services, University of Michigan.

"Don't Be Blindsided by Recruiters' Questions" by Perri Capell, *CareerJournal.com* (March 29, 2004).

In the Company of Giants: Candid Conversations with the Visionaries of the Digital World (Reprint edition) by Rama Dev Jager and Ortiz Rafael (McGraw-Hill, 1998).

Topgrading by Bradford Smart (Portfolio, 2005).

"More Employers Are Using Personality Tests as Hiring Tools" by Victoria Knight, *Wall Street Journal Online* (March 21, 2006).

"Employers Gauge Candidates' Skills At 'Real-World' Tasks" by Erin White, *Wall Street Journal Online* (January 16, 2006).

"Variable Pay Programs Provide Flexibility, Incentives" by Joan Lloyd, Joanlloyd.com (February 4, 1996).

"Skill Based Pay: A Brief Overview" Effectivecompensation.com (2003).

"The Family and Medical Leave Act of 1993," U.S. Department of Labor Fact Sheet No. 28, dol.gov. (December 5, 2006).

"Making the Case for Telecommuting" by Jill Hamburg Coplan, *BusinessWeek Online* (April 2001).`

"Why Small Businesses Pay Less" Salary.com (2006).

"Small Business Secrets to Hiring" by Karen E. Klein, *BusinessWeek Online* (August 14, 2006).

"Strings Attached" by Jonathan A. Segal, *Human Resources* (February 2005).

"Let's Hear It for B Players" by Thomas J. DeLong, *Harvard Business Review* (June 2003).

"Survey Reveals Top 5 Mistakes Companies Make When Hiring or Promoting," Right Management (June 12, 2006).

"The Wegmans Way" by Matthew Boyle, *Fortune* (January 2005).

"New Practice Offers to Support Entry-level New Hires," Northrop Grumman *Currents* newsletter (August 2003).

Recommended Reading

Hire with Your Head: Using Power Hiring to Build Great Teams, 2nd edition
Lou Adler
How to recruit, interview, and hire the best people for the job.

The Transparent Leader: How to Build a Great Company Through Straight Talk, Openness, and Accountability
Herb Baum with Tammy Kling
In the wake of numerous corporate scandals, Baum offers business leaders a compelling method to get maximum results by being open and honest in business practices.

Leaders: Strategies for Taking Charge, 2nd edition
Warren Bennis and Burt Nanus
Leadership guru Warren Bennis and his coauthor Burt Nanus reveal the four key principles every manager should know.

Reinventing Leadership: Strategies to Empower the Organization
Warren Bennis and Robert Townsend
Two of America's foremost experts on leadership show how their strategies can lead organizations into a future that includes better employees with increased employee satisfaction and continued economic growth.

The One Minute Manager Builds High Performing Teams
Ken Blanchard, Eunice Parisi-Carew, and Donald Carew
Blanchard and company show how to develop any group
into a successful team with efficiency and minimal stress.

*First, Break All the Rules: What the World's Greatest
Managers Do Differently*
Marcus Buckingham and Curt Coffman
This book presents four management keys to help managers do a better job of hiring, evaluating, promoting and,
if necessary, firing employees. Learn how to find the right
fit for employees, focus on their strengths, define desired
results, and select people with talent.

Now, Discover Your Strengths
Marcus Buckingham and Donald O. Cliffton, Ph.D.
This book encourages managers to increase performance
by focusing on employees' strengths rather than improving
their weaknesses.

*The Success Principles™: How to Get from Where You Are
to Where You Want to Be*
Jack Canfield with Janet Switzer
One of the coauthors of the incredibly successful *Chicken
Soup for the Soul* series provides the principles and strate-
gies to meet a wide variety of goals.

*Good to Great: Why Some Companies Make the Leap . . .
and Others Don't*
Jim Collins
The findings from *Good to Great* will surprise many readers
and shed light on virtually every area of management strategy and practice.

The Effective Executive
Peter F. Drucker
Drucker, one of the great authorities on the art and science
of management, shows how to "get the right things done,"
demonstrating the distinctive skill of the executive and
offering fresh insights into old and seemingly obvious business situations.

Innovation and Entrepreneurship
Peter F. Drucker
This is the classic business tome for presenting innovation and entrepreneurship as a purposeful and systematic discipline. This practical book explains what all businesses and institutions have to know, learn, and do in today's market.

The Practice of Management
Peter F. Drucker
The first book to depict management as a distinct function and to recognize managing as a separate responsibility, this classic Drucker work is the fundamental and basic book for understanding these ideas.

The Daily Drucker: 366 Days of Insight and Motivation for Getting the Right Things Done
Peter F. Drucker with Joseph A. Maciariello
Drucker offers his penetrating and practical wisdom with his trademark clarity, vision, and humanity. *The Daily Drucker* provides the inspiration and advice to meet life's many challenges.

Corps Business: The 30 Management Principles of the U.S. Marines
David H. Freedman
Freeman examines the organization and culture of the United States Marine Corps and relates how business enterprises could benefit from such Marine values as sacrifice, perseverance, integrity, commitment, and loyalty.

The Girl's Guide to Starting Your Own Business: Candid Advice, Frank Talk, and True Stories for the Successful Entrepreneur
Caitlin Friedman and Kimberly Yorio
Geared toward challenges faced by self-employed businesswomen, *The Girl's Guide to Starting Your Own Business* offers solutions and advice for handling a range of issues, including how to hire employees.

The Big Book of Small Business: You Don't Have to Run Your Business by the Seat of Your Pants
Tom Gegax with Phil Bolsta
This book includes essential information on planning for growth, hiring the best people, and maximizing their potential.

*The E-Myth Manager: Why Most Managers Aren't Effective
and What to Do About It*
Michael E. Gerber
Drawing on lessons learned from working with more than
15,000 small, medium-sized, and very large organizations,
Gerber reveals why management doesn't work—and what to
do about it.

*Common Sense Business: Starting, Operating, and Growing
Your Small Business in Any Economy!*
Steve Gottry
This book tells you how to succeed throughout every phase
of the small business life cycle—from starting to operating,
growing, and even closing down a business. Author Gottry
offers practical tips on hiring.

Breaking the Bamboo Ceiling: Career Strategies for Asians
Jane Hyun
Using case studies, interviews, and anecdotes, Hyun iden-
tifies issues and provides strategies for Asian Americans to
succeed in corporate America. An interesting analysis of
cultural differences.

*It's Not the Big That Eat the Small . . . It's the Fast That
Eat the Slow: How to Use Speed as a Competitive Tool in
Business*
Jason Jennings and Laurence Haughton
Instructive text on how to create strategic planning and
creativity to speed your business efficiently past the
competition.

"Yes" or "No": The Guide to Better Decisions
Spencer Johnson, M.D.
Bestselling author Spencer Johnson presents a practical
system anyone can use to make better decisions, soon and
often—both at work and in personal life.

*The Wisdom of Teams: Creating the High Performance
Organization*
Jon R. Katzenbach and Douglas K. Smith
Authors Katzenbach and Smith reveal the most important
element in team success, who excels at team leadership,
and why company-wide change depends on teams.

Hire Tough, Manage Easy: How to Find and Hire the Best Hourly Employees
Mel Kleinman
This practical guide offers practical advice on getting the best hourly employees and how to go about finding, recruiting, and hiring the best candidates.

Swim with the Sharks without Being Eaten Alive: Outsell, Outmanage, Outmotivate, and Outnegotiate Your Competition
Harvey B. Mackay
In this straight-from-the-hip handbook, with almost 2 million in print, bestselling author and self-made millionaire Mackay reviews the secrets of his success.

You Can't Win a Fight with Your Boss: & 55 Other Rules for Success
Tom Markert
This guide to surviving the pitfalls of the modern corporate environment presents 56 practical rules that one can use to find corporate success.

Executive Intelligence: What All Great Leaders Have
Justin Menkes
In this thought-provoking volume, Menkes pinpoints the cognitive skills needed to thrive in senior management positions.

The Corporate Coach: How to Build a Team of Loyal Customers and Happy Employees
James B. Miller with Paul B. Brown
Founder and CEO of Miller Business Systems, Jim Miller shows how giving customers legendary services and also motivating employees makes for a winning combination.

In Search of Excellence: Lessons from America's Best-Run Companies
Thomas J. Peters and Robert H. Waterman, Jr.
Based on a study of 43 of America's best-run companies from a diverse array of business sectors, *In Search of Excellence* describes eight basic principles of management that made these organizations successful.

Quiet Leadership: Six Steps to Transforming Performance at Work
David Rock
Rock demonstrates how to be a quiet leader, master at bringing out the best performance in others, by improving the way people process information.

Topgrading: How Leading Companies Win by Hiring, Coaching, and Keeping the Best People
Bradford Smart
This book argues that an essential component of growing and maintaining a company is the ability to find, recruit, and retain superior personnel.

The Cycle of Leadership: How Great Leaders Teach Their Companies to Win
Noel M. Tichy
Using examples from real companies, Tichy shows how managers can begin to transform their own businesses into teaching organizations and, consequently, better-performing companies with better-performing employees.

The Leadership Engine: How Winning Companies Build Leaders at Every Level
Noel M. Tichy
A framework for developing leaders at all levels of an organization helps to develop the next generation of leaders so that a company can grow from within, which is the key to excellence, stability, and building team loyalty.

The Visionary's Handbook: Nine Paradoxes That Will Shape the Future of Your Business
Watts Wacker and Jim Taylor with Howard Means
This book presents a vision of the present and future to create a course for the future based upon the authors' understanding of nine paradoxes that define the world's business and social climates.

Winning
Jack Welch with Suzy Welch
The core of *Winning* is devoted to the real "stuff" of work. Packed with personal anecdotes, this book offers deep insights, original thinking, and solutions to nuts-and-bolts problems.

Index

A
Academic record check, 92
Adler, Lou, 32
advertising, 11–29
  classified ads, 14
  costs, 20
  Internet, 16–20
    job boards, 16
    company Web site, 19, 30
  newspaper, 16–20, 23
  print v. Internet, 17
  writing your ad, 24–29
Alsop, Ronald, 43
Anderson, Jenny, 13
assessment tests, as predic-
       tors of performance,
       90–95

B
Babcock, Pamela, 85
background checks, 84, 88–95
Baum, Herb, 72
benefits, 11, 106–113
bonuses, 102–103
Booz Allen Hamilton, 22
Bossidy, Larry, 98
Buckingham, Marcus, 124

C
Capell, Perri, 45, 75
certifications and licenses, 11
checking references, 87–90
Clinton, Bill, 81
Collins, Jim, 88
credit checks, 89, 90
criminal checks, 84–85, 89–90

D
databases, 14, 19, 23, 30, 53
  management tools, 14
  searching, 53
DaimerChrysler, 95
Davis, Martin E., 67
differentiated compensation,
    130
discrimination, 77–80,
diversity, 13
Drucker, Peter, x, 76, 120

E
Economy, Peter, 63

F
Family and Medical Leave Act
    of 1993 (FMLA), 107
flexible schedules, 111–114,
    130
follow-up interviews, 86–87

G
Google, 23, 77, 83, 108

H
Hanson, Fay, 28
Haughton, Laurence, 25
Hyatt, Josh, 64

I
internships, 36–41
  managing interns, 41
Internet advertising, 16–29
interviewing
  as a team, 83
  basics, 62
  behavior-based
    interviewing, 68,
    69–74
  discriminatory questions,
    77–80, 86–87
  documenting, 82
  entry-level candidates, 75
  follow-up, 86–88
  phone, 58
  standard questions, 65
  types of interviews, 80–82
I.Q. tests, 92–93

J
Jennings, Jason, 25
job applications, 47, 60–61
job boards, 16–20, 22–24
job descriptions, 3–11, 20, 24,
  53, 64
job fairs, 41–42
job requirements, 8, 10, 62
  physical requirements, 11
  required working hours, 11
job simulations, 95–96

K
Klein, Karen E., 115
Kleinman, Mel, 129
Knight, Victoria, 87

L
Lefkow, Dave, 33
litigation, 120
Lloyd, Joan, 105

M
Mackay, Harvey B., 6–7, 101
Mcnkcs, Justin, 68, 82
Microsoft, 83
MySQL, 64

N
Nelson, Bob, 63

O
Occupational Safety and
    Health Administra-
    tion (OSHA), 122
online ads, 24–29
orientations for new
    employees, 9,
    121–125

P
pension plans, 108–111
performance management
    cycle, 125–127
perks, 111–114
personality tests, 90–95
Peters, Thomas J., 14, 57
preliminary screening, 19,
    56–62
  in-store automated sys-
    tems, 60
  knowledge tests, 62
Procter & Gamble, 130
Prystay, Cris, 15

R
recruiting, 22, 29–32, 42–47,
    123
  job fairs, 41
  contingency firms, 44
  retainer firms, 44
  Directory of Executive
    Recruiters, 47
references, 86, 87–90

referrals, 22, 32–36
  alumni referrals and rehires, 36
  employee referrals, 33, 34–36
resumes, 47–53
  evaluating, 47
  red flags, 48
  responding to, 29
  sorting, 53
  types, 52
retaining employees, 9, 127–130
  feedback, 129
  motivation, 129

S

salary, 8, 11, 24, 26, 40, 44, 58, 61, 91, 96, 100–105, 109–111, 116, 118, 128
  alternatives, 104
  expectations, 51
  offers, 100–102
  variable pay programs, 104
Schmidt, Eric, 77

screening, 56–62
Segal, Jonathan A., 119
Sloan, Alfred, 58
Smart, Bradford, 90
Spherion Corporation, 59, 89
Springer, Karen, 9
Starbucks, 18
Swisher, Larry, 17

T

Taylor, William C., 12
termination, 131–132
Torre, Joe, 117

W

Waterman, Jr, Robert H., 57
Web site as recruiting tool, 30–32
Weddle, Peter, 35
Wegmans, 126–127
Welch, Jack, 4, 5, 54, 66
White, Erin, 95

Z

Zimmerman, Eileen, 39

Make sure you have all the Best Practices!

COLLINS BEST PRACTICES

Achieving GOALS

Define and Surpass Your
High Performance Goals

KATHLEEN SCHIENLE

Best Practices: Achieving Goals
ISBN: 978-0-06-114574-2

COLLINS BEST PRACTICES

Communicating EFFECTIVELY

Write, Speak, and Present
with Authority

GARRY KRANZ

Best Practices: Communicating Effectively
ISBN: 978-0-06-114568-1

COLLINS BEST PRACTICES

Difficult PEOPLE

Working Effectively with
Prickly Bosses, Co-Workers,
and Clients

JOHN HOOVER

Best Practices: Difficult People
ISBN: 978-0-06-114559-9

COLLINS BEST PRACTICES

Evaluating PERFORMANCE

How to Appraise,
Promote, and Fire

BARRY SILVERSTEIN

Best Practices: Evaluating Performance
ISBN: 978-0-06-114560-5

Make sure you have all the Best Practices!

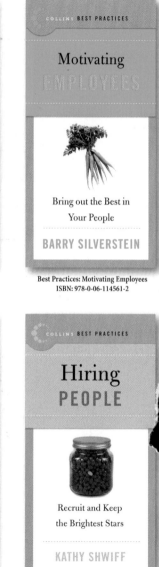